Uncomfortably Numb

How the Verbally Abusive
Relationship can slowly
Numb Your Soul

By Laurie Ault, CAS

Dedicated to my sons

Brandon and Jon

Who have been my real teachers

Printed in the United States of America

Because of the dynamic nature of the internet any Web addresses or links contained in this book may have changed since publication and may no longer be valid.

Prologue
Intention

I found my way out of a verbally abusive relationship. Because it was a huge learning experience I felt compelled to share what was and still is a very personal part of my past life. I truly want to help anyone who has never experienced this type of relationship to be able to see it when it is standing right in front of you. And to avoid it. My intention for this book is to reach an audience of women who have not yet made irrevocable mistakes in choosing a partner or mate. Or if they have chosen someone that diminishes them in some way that in these pages they may find the ability to recognize themselves and their partner or their relationship dynamics. It is my hope that this book will minimize time wasted in recognizing a verbally abusive relationship that could become at its worst a physically abusive relationship.

I have attempted to tell a short version about my own experience with verbal abuse. I wanted to describe what a verbally abusive relationship looks like. I have tried to keep it short and to the point and as uncomplicated as possible to make it easy to read, digest and examine. There are lots of self-help books out that can make it complicated. I just wanted to talk to you. I want to keep it simple.

Verbal Abuse is overlooked frequently in society and it is my belief we have in many ways become almost deaf to it especially when it comes to how it relates to women. In society we have become conditioned and so disregard what we are hearing especially in the media, in sitcoms and commercials on television as many look to these sources for examples to model their own behaviors. Social Media now plays a part in what young women are exposed to as they are conditioned and sometimes learn that what is shown are the ways to behave. Put downs and negative role models are what seem "normal." This can make verbal abuse harder to recognize. No one deserves to be treated with disrespect from anyone anywhere ever. Most certainly we do not deserve this type of treatment in our own homes in our most intimate relationships with husbands, boyfriends and partners.

It took me far too long to find my way out of the situation, life, marriage I had signed up for. The stories I tell are very personal. They have happened to many. Of this I am certain. The details may be different, but the actions are deliberate by the abuser and the results are the same. Sadness, confusion, depression, and the list is long of the effects of verbal abuse. Especially over time in a long term relationship. I am hoping that this book can be somewhat of a handbook for warning signs of verbal and physical abuse. I have tried to be direct and straightforward in telling about parts of my life that when lived were the most excruciating of times in my life. On occasion I still recall the pain of the past and choose not to access the feelings associated with it. It is past, it is over and I will never go back there. I have suffered with Post Traumatic Stress and have fought it. I have actively worked with counselors and others to remove these patterns from my life. I left the situation once and for all 18 years ago and it took three years from the time of separation to divorce.   I have survival scars which provide me a determination to feel my feelings, and to experience life at its' fullest.

A labor of love

At first this book was a labor of catharsis, I needed to get this experience out of my cells out of my being so that I would not hold any pain inside me anymore.   I would write whenever I felt the urge in bits and pieces. Until one day, I finally wrote that there was no longer any reaction to any words spoken to me from my abuser.

Writing this became a labor of helping. I wanted to write this to possibly help someone, anyone from having to repeat my very painful experiences for themselves. At the very least I wanted to help someone in the figuring out part of how to gain freedom from this type of relationship. I do not wish this experience on any woman. Life is short. No one needs to waste precious time living in this type of nightmare. And then finally, at long last, it became a labor of love. Love that I had finally learned to give myself. I had learned enough to at last let this go, to free my soul and let myself reach once again for my own dreams.

Acknowledgments

First I must truly thank my husband Tim for his many years of actively listening to me, and in so doing really getting to know me better than anyone on this planet does. I must also thank him for giving me generously the time I needed to write, to process and move through a negative experience in my past. What a gift he has been to me. He has encouraged me to grow even though the passage took me away from moments spent in the now. Thank you Tim you are my best friend.

Thank you to my sons now grown. You have taught me so much. About the world, about humanity, about myself, and ultimately about yourselves. You are/were my learning curve on what is genuinely wonderful about boys who become men. You taught me that my job was to try and teach you to respect yourselves and others, which meant ALL others equally. You are both generous of spirit. I knew what being a girl and then a woman meant. And then I had the two of you to teach me every step of the way. I truly appreciate what good men there are in this world. My sons are two of them. I am grateful for you both.

I had no compass when it came to identifying with boys because I am not one. I got what I needed in this life to learn. I have two brothers, two sons, two nephews and am typically the lone female at dinners in my home. For twenty years we had no females added to our family. So if you mistake my crusade for equality and an equal voice for complaints about men, those are legitimate concerns. I also know the other side of the coin which is where men are as wonderful a creature as the best of women are. They do exist and they are here on this planet with us. (Keep your sense of humor). I now have a grandson as well. I have been fortunate. I have two granddaughters who know they are equally as smart and have many gifts just like their brother does.

Thank you to Joyful Heart Foundation, Victims of Crime, The World Health Organization, The Feminist Majority, Soroptimist International, and in addition the list is endless when it comes to women's organizations, Domestic Abuse Organizations across the country as well as other agencies including the courts who work to help women find themselves and to move on to a better life. Advocates for women are out there and I am appreciative and thankful.

I have to also thank Jan and Colleen, both therapists who early on helped me to save my life. They helped me grow up and inspired me to become whole no matter how much it took and how long we worked on this endeavor. They spoke to me at a level of understanding that accelerated my growth. I have always sought to become the best version of myself on a daily basis. Sometimes that translated to minute by minute. Thank you, the debt cannot be repaid.

Thank you for taking the time to read this publication. I hope it can help or will help any who are experiencing these issues currently or who are contemplating leaving a situation like the one I, and many others have experienced.

You are not alone. And…It's not your fault.

Table of Contents

Introduction

In the telling of my story, in telling what I have learned, time wasted, time recovered, the losing of most of myself, and then of finding me again, remembering who I was and am in full measure has driven me to share my experiences with others hoping any time lost can be minimized. I wanted to share my experiences in particular with those of you who have walked in my shoes. Mostly I want you to know that you are not crazy, you are not alone. The existence of discrimination against women, and verbal abuse in particular is alive and well today. I could rant for quite some time about inequality for women historically, and the fact that discrimination still exists today everywhere and in every country including the United States of America. That subject alone could be and is the subject of many, many books. The fact that human trafficking is allowed all over the world is cause to write a book about the injustices perpetrated against women and others every day.

I find myself now looking back over time at my own life and the lessons it held for me. I began writing this book in 2013. I had seen a program that had aired a piece about a man named Booker Wright. A black man from Mississippi who stood as an example at great risk to himself in 1960's Mississippi for speaking out about the way he was treated by white men. Mr. Wright was shown in a short clip in a documentary called "Mississippi A Self Portrait." Mr. Wright consented to be in this film to talk about his role as a waiter in a restaurant that served all white men.

After watching Mr. Wright talk about what was on the menu in a lyrical way in more of his (negro) black man persona, he switches while speaking to us to a serious and authentic man who doesn't want his children to live the way he has had to, he hopes for them an education and a way to live that does not include being treated as less important. He does not want his children to be treated with discrimination because of the color of their skin. As you read this description do not forget to factor in the context of the times.

As I watched and listened, it hit me to my core that I understood exactly what Mr. Wright was talking about because of the similar discrimination shown to women of every color. I understand this man's feelings because I know what this feels like. I have not walked a mile in the same shoes, but I have walked a mile in similar shoes. Discrimination is discrimination.

To be treated differently, to be discriminated against merely because I am a female, and living in this country for 50 plus years as a woman is like Mr. Wrights experience in many ways. At least if you are black in 2018 it is not politically correct to publically put down black people any longer. But, it is still ok to degrade, objectify, subjugate, verbally abuse, physically abuse and use women for entertainment any way the media or others decide to. Until recently. The cry from women and others who support them right now in this the first year after Trump became President is becoming louder and louder. Thank goodness. Can real lasting change happen now?

Women tried to tell the world about these issues and inequities in the 1960's and on into the 1970's. I was energized and encouraged. I was a feminist at age 20 and was ready for the Equal Rights Amendment to be passed. The Equal Rights Amendment was not passed and it still sits all these years later as unfinished business. And then somewhere along the way it got quiet again, the status quo seemed easier. The visible changes made were few in retrospect. Yes, more women joined the work force and became visible, but all of the underlying issues remained.

Now it is almost 50 years later. We will have the same conversations again. The power struggle and wrestling match, the battle between the sexes has begun in earnest again. So what will change? What will be won? When the calmness and quiet return and we feel we have made strides and effected change that will last, will we really have won anything in the end that will truly make a difference for women not only here in the United States of America, but globally? All of these things will be discussed and analyzed, broken down and looked at. This book will only touch on this part of the subject matter because I really want to communicate basic information about how to discuss the reality of verbal abuse. I believe that if lasting change in any avenue related to women is to happen and remain we must know where the roots of these behaviors begin. How do men learn them and how can we change how we think about each other, and then how we ultimately treat each other?

Because our children look to the media more than ever before in our history are we going back in time 100 years in our messages about how we should treat each other? I have been horrified at what I am seeing and hearing. This subject is also one that an entire book could be written about. In great detail I could describe what is wrong in our society today that allows this type of treatment, even this type of spectacle of women to be ok in main stream society. Music Videos, Movies, magazine and television advertising, all of the messages fed to our young men and women, to our children seems to have slipped by many of us. We have seemingly become desensitized to this takeover of teaching our children who they have the possibility to become, what their roles are and what acceptable ways of treating each other and interacting are. 'Perhaps this is part of the collateral damage provided by social media.

What drives me most, first and foremost is what the actual effect of being treated as less than, less important, less smart, less human is having on the world and individually on females today. It is my message that it is not ok ever, to accept being put down verbally, talked down to, patronized, harassed, discriminated against by anyone and most certainly it is not ok to be treated this way by a partner, the person who is supposed to love you. This book is about women because I am one. I am certain the statistics on women abusing men are much higher than reported so this type of unacceptable treatment can be perpetrated by either sex against one another. However, it is my belief that women are treated in a discriminatory fashion more often than men. This has been my own experience. I am afraid that in the next few generations we are and may be taking a step back in time and it will take another 50 years to recover from this dangerous and unacceptable path. Unless…we follow the conversation currently started in 2017-18 through to conclusion. Asking for specific changes making sure we can implement them. Education is key.

This book is about abuse. Abuse verbally, physically, and the damage it does to your mind, soul and your body. How its effects distort your thinking, how over time its insidious effects try to take your life from you. Even small statements made by a partner that seem harmless are actually harmful, not only to you but to your children if you have them. I am hopeful that my story, my thoughts will help you avoid this type of partner. Maybe my story will help you recognize what you are really dealing with before you make the mistake of committing to a life with this type of partner.

My life with a verbal abuser left me feeling off balance and confused for longer than I would like to admit. When recovering from this experience I wrote:

"It was almost like being hit upside the head and what results is a view of the world that is black and white, off balance, with the vision in one eye gone...

No depth or deep dimensions, no color. No real hearing anymore, just buzzing inside my head. Words, they are as if I am hearing them from far away, echoes in a tunnel or mumbling that almost makes sense.

 Now, at last my world has come back to color, three dimensions with detail. My numbness which served me well has melted and become a wonderful feeling on my skin. I now feel the warmth of the sun, the delicious coldness of swimming in the lake, the colors and textures of living that once were gone. Everything had become too painful to see, to hear and to feel. I had become "Uncomfortably Numb."

Chapter One
The Numbing of a Soul

I ask myself how did this happen? Part of this numbing of me happened because of when I was born. The expected roles for girls and women from the late 1950's had not yet evolved. Women's Liberation had not yet arrived. In today's world I am concerned that even though girls and women know there are many different options on how to live their lives what the media shows them, shows all of us are the same old patterns about where their usefulness really lies. The media shows women in every way how we are to look, how we are to behave, and what we can brush off and try to ignore.

When we are spoken to in disrespectful ways we are taught to overlook it. At least we were in my lifetime. Women are shown as a spectacle to be stared at and to be judged. The messages in commercials streaming nonstop are about our sexuality, that this is where our power lies and nowhere else. We know this is not true, but these are many messages seen and heard daily.

Growing up in my family dynamic, sandwiched between two brothers I was keenly aware from the moment I got to the planet that I was treated differently from them. I had no idea why this was so. It just was. It did not take me long to note that they got to stand up in front of the toilet and I did not. I could not fathom why anyone would treat me as less smart, less important or less in any way just because I chose not to stand up to pee and I had different body parts. In school testing I scored approximately the same as my brothers and it was a pretty level playing field when it came to brains. Why then was I given all of the household duties and they were given none? No one ever said anything verbally that would have led me to the conclusion that my role was to be so different from my brothers. Actions speak louder than words. Back in the early 60's women served men dinner first bringing them the best cuts of meat. When my mom and I could finally sit down at the table our food was not so hot anymore. To this day I prefer my food steaming hot.

The social conditioning, I received was not meant to damage me really it was just the way things were back then. This is what made it feel "normal" to me when I became a young woman to bring coffee to my boss. The conditioning I lived through as a young girl made me stronger in some ways. When I was told I could not do something I would set out to prove that I could and would. When my brothers climbed trees I would also climbing as high or higher than they. I would set out to beat them in any way possible. I clearly remember playing checkers with my brother and winning. He was so angry. I was supposed to let him win. I knew this without having been told. I would not and could not do that. I always did my best and if that meant winning at checkers so be it. I would play him over and over again and win if I had played the best match.

I did not care if he got upset. I did not believe in letting him win just because he was a guy. The trouble is my brother never played me again after that one game.

When I was in about the fifth grade I recall so vividly playing tether ball on the playground at recess. I loved to play tetherball. I played this one boy giving it all I had. I won the game fair and square having been the superior player. If you have ever played this game you know that if you can hit the ball that is attached to the rope high enough and hard enough over your opponents head the ball will wrap around the pole at lightning speed and win you the game. This is what I did. When the boy realized I had just won, (just kicked his butt) he wound up his fist and punched me squarely in the stomach. He hit me so hard he knocked out every granule of air in my lungs. I could not move until I could finally catch my breath. I could not believe he was such a sore loser. His pride was hurt because I had won in front of his friends. I admit it I told the yard teacher and to add insult to injury so to speak the boy was now in trouble for hitting me and had to go talk to the principal.

From the moment I looked around as a small child, I could not believe that the rules were set up so that my brothers had more of an advantage in this life. Free white men they were to become. I do not mean this as an insult, only as a fact because the lens these men see everything through is the lens of just that, men of privilege in our society. I was told that my choices for career were nurse, teacher or secretary. The thought of any of those choices at the time bothered me. What if I did not want to be any of those things? They are all fine professions, but why did I not hear Doctor, Lawyer, Astronaut or President or all of the choices there are today? Narrow thinking about gender roles was the message.

Oh... and I was supposed to get married and have children, be a mom. I was lucky to have a grandmother who was ahead of her time and throughout my childhood would say to me as she rocked back and forth in her chair. :Lawrie (Laurie) she was from the south, "Don't ever depend on any man. Make sure you have a career and that you can be independent. Have something you can fall back on if you need to." Then she would cite examples like my mother who had gone back to school when I was five to become a nurse. My grandmother was a teacher. She worked all of her life until she retired. That way she had her own money and did not have to answer to anyone about every dime she spent.   She did not have kids until she was 29 and 31. In the 1930's this was not the trend. She was ahead of her time.   When she had her two children she learned how hard it was to work and care for them well. She had no help at all from my grandfather of course. Raising children was a woman's job after all.

My grandmother never wanted me to be "stuck" with any man. She believed in independence. She also said "Lawrie, (Laurie) you can just as easily love a rich man as a poor one." This may have been true, but I was never smart enough to take this advice to heart! I was always proud that I had married for love. Three times. So much for marrying for money. As it turns out it might have been something I would have liked to try.

The other side of this equation was that I was also being taught how to do my nails, how to keep my hands moisturized, how to be a girl which included how to keep peace in the family. My grandmother was to tell me many things as she rocked back and forth in her chair. What I was not taught were boundaries. I was taught to please and appease. I had no boundaries, no sense of where I was, where I began and ended and another person began.

Because I am female I was taught to do everything for everyone else first. You give to your family; you give to anyone who needs something and when you are done you get to be you. By the time you get to you, you may have never learned who and what you are. I became so intermingled with others, more specifically men that I almost lost myself entirely. As women many of us are taught to give ourselves away. To give up everything for another. In my journey there has always been a piece of myself, however small that I kept for myself. A small piece that carried my identity, my dreams for myself, my essence, all of the components that made me a strong, independent woman. I never gave everything away. I put it on hold, let everything else eclipse what I wanted, I put off being me.

I did not realize it until after it was done, but that is what happened. Because I did not have boundaries and to me a "normal" way of living was to give, to serve, to help others first. First and foremost, give to your husband, your children, your job, and your community. After all of the giving it took me a very long time to fully become me.

Because of the time in history that it was, (the 1960's) the dynamic in many families for many who grew up then, it was "normal" to put up with all kinds of dysfunction. Those were the times. Many did not "use their words" to resolve conflict or discuss anything. We did not discuss anything. Suffice it to say that I believe in the words from John Mayer's song lyrics telling fathers and mothers to be kind to their daughters. It always matters how we act and act out. There can be a disconnect between some fathers and daughters. Many of us have had and do have our "daddy issues." We either resolve them or we don't. Sometimes it can take a lifetime to do so.

In my case, I thought that if I ever did anything well enough I would be loved in a real and meaningful way by a man. I wanted to make my parents, and in particular my father proud of me. I wanted my parents to know me. If I could or would ever be good enough to have my father "see" me, know me, if I could feel as though I was important to him then I would be happy. Somehow this translated to my relationships with men. Surprise, Surprise.   This is not uncommon for many daughters. My parents divorced when I was almost 15.

I mentioned I have been married three times. I have been married for most of my adult life. When I was a teenager I dated different people and one thing seemed to pop up in what was to become a pattern for me. That is that what was most important was that the guy liked me. Not so important was that I liked him. I also found guys who were funny and made me laugh. In more than one of my relationships I would end up with a guy and then a man who did not really value me as a separate, intricate, unique human being with rights and thoughts of my own.

In one of my relationships I was to learn about myself in great depth, I was to learn first that my picker was damaged. When I would pick a man to be with thinking I was head over heels in love and that this could be "the one" I was to learn that my picker was definitely not working well. I want to tell you about some of the components that were key to my learning and that took place within several of the relationships I was to have from the time I was fifteen and throughout my life.

If you want to join with another, have a boyfriend, a partner, a marriage, my advice to you is to make sure you know who and what you are looking at. The kind of life you will have depends completely on who you choose to be with. We have all heard the comments about not surrounding yourself with negative people and hanging out with people you love and that love you. But, when it comes to choosing a mate this person sometimes seems to be exempt from our scrutiny. We don't ask ourselves many important questions about how this person is. How they fit into our world and most important is how they treat us and how they will treat us in a long term relationship. Sounds like a no brainer right? So, along the way I found myself in a relationship with a guy I will call Sam. I thought I was head over heels in love. I had never felt this way about someone. I was determined to give everything to this relationship. I almost did.

Chapter Two
Power and Control

After I became involved with Sam first as a friend and then as a partner I have to say that confusion is the word that describes the next several years. I had known Sam as a friend for seven years before we dated. I thought I knew what I needed to know about Sam. I thought we both felt the same way. What I did not know was that seldom do two people love each other in the same way. I thought that Sam felt about me, the way I felt about him. I lived in magical thinking for a long time. To be fair to me, I am not a stupid woman; I was just immature emotionally and saw what I needed to see.

When two people enter a relationship they are typically on their best behavior in the beginning. We try to show ourselves to our potential mate in the best ways possible. Sam was to have even more of an advantage because he was almost thirteen years older than I. He had also been married previously for seventeen years and had two children. He also had plenty of time to hone his skills in a marriage context. He was pretty darn good at the wrestling match we were to have for the next fifteen years. This man had learned to sell anything to anyone and was extremely good at it. In my case Sam sold me a man that did not exist. He sold me a man who believed women were equal and of value. He said he believed that women could do any job well. He sold me a man who said he wanted to be my partner.

As it turned out, Sam had portrayed himself as many, many things that were not true. I had always thought I had a good sense about people. I had instincts about who was real or not, who was good or not. I was so young when I met this man, so naïve. I had yet to discover all of who I was. Ultimately, my family was impressed by Sam, approved of Sam and thought I would be a fool not to stay with him. Sam had sold my family on his persona; his ability to make lots of money was enough for many in my family to believe he was the right choice for me. I was led to believe if there were problems in this relationship it could not just be Sam who was at fault, at the very least I had to share in the issues that initially had threatened to make us go our own separate ways. So, I toughed it out and gave more.

It was interesting to me to discover that even though I knew this man for 8 years by the time we were married I literally said "Uh-oh" before noon the day after our wedding.   I hate to be cliché' about the personality issues that were Sam, but I must refer to Dr. Jeckel and Mr. Hyde. To make a long story short and to cut to the chase, this dynamic was to define our relationship and my confusion for way too long into the future.

In public, Sam was a most charismatic personality. He knew how to impress people and to make them like him. He wanted to have many friends, especially male friends who would buy into his successful image of himself. He made people believe he was a kind, caring, good man. This was the persona I fell in love with.

At home, he was about power and control. He wanted power over me and my small son. Sam set about making the two of us feel insignificant and small; attacking any self-esteem we would manage to gather on a daily basis. This confused me because the man Sam had sold me had told me he believed women were smart and of value. At home, the other persona ruled. I was puzzled, knocked off balance by this behavior. I tried to do everything better. I took on more and more responsibility.

I had started a business and Sam joined me in it. We worked very well together. We became very successful. I realized that everyone we knew believed that Sam had started our business and that I had just joined him in it and worked with him in it. The reverse was true. It was my (our) business and I ran every aspect of it. Sam was great at selling. I sold as well. We were a good business team. This is the reason our life together lasted so long. Our business relationship worked for quite some time. The other parts at home that were supposed to include love, affection and real care for each other became less and less. This was not good.

I had committed myself to this partnership. For a very long time I could not quite put my finger on why I felt bad frequently. Eventually I was to ask myself, why do I feel so badly? Sam doesn't hit me. So what could be wrong? I decided to begin therapy so that I could understand myself better. I spent the next three years talking with my wonderful counselor trying to grow up emotionally. I would tell her things that bothered me during each week. In the telling, she would hear something that Sam had said to me that week looking surprised, saying "He said that to you?" What she was hearing were all of the ways that Sam would verbally abuse me each day.

This verbal abuse was insidious, disguised, and seemingly a normal way to converse with my mate. I could not recognize this type of abuse because it was something I had become conditioned to as a child. In the conditioning I received in my childhood about the ways women (girls) were to be treated and what my role was to be I did not realize what verbal abuse was in everyday life. I was taught to be nice and to appease. This is where some of us were taught to overlook the behavior of others and those who may have power over us. I was always puzzled when a playmate or a sibling did not treat me very well or did not live by the golden rule as I thought people did. Teaching young women or girls to overlook how they are treated in the silence of being a "nice" girl is where the conditioning begins.

What I was to learn in the next few years in therapy was there are two kinds of power. The first is Power Over another, the second is Personal Power. In my relationship with Sam he was all about having power and control over me and by proxy my small son. I slowly began to lose my personal power. The way the world is set up ironically, and not surprisingly is so that a few may have power over many. The insides of conflict as we have always known it are about power and control. When this happens in a marriage, partnership and in relationships with children the results can be and are devastating. Especially to those who are controlled by means of physical and verbal abuse. Verbal abuse is more disguised but is no less damaging to the soul. The scars are not visible on the skin, but under the surface in our souls and looking out at the world through our eyes, the pain, anguish and numbing of spirit is visible to the naked eye. If anyone cares to see. If you look in the mirror at yourself and this is who is looking back at you, if your mate or partner inflicts wounds with words and actions you must ask for change, you must ask for it to stop.

It is my belief that some of the messages we receive in society that women are objects, that our only real worth lies in our sexuality and in what we can do for our men that this is the beginning of abuse of power and control. These are the roots and beginnings of verbal abuse, of not being valued as human beings. For a very long time in our society women were only seen as extensions of men. In many ways this can still be said to be true.

The messages and conditioning that happen every day from others, from TV and music videos, lyrics to current songs, messages in movies and comedies under the guise of "It was just a joke" are the beginnings of where we as a society think it is still ok to put women down, to devalue and abuse women in our thinking, in our actions, in our words and then in our fists. Women are treated as second class citizens everywhere, every day. We must ask for it to stop. We must make our voices heard. Black men and women did this during the civil rights movement of the 1960's. Women did this in the 1920's when demanding the right to vote. This did not guarantee equality and still does not.

Women asked for change in the 1970's. We made some progress. Now, in 2018 men are still running the world. That is fine, but many want to return to times past. This is my real concern. It seems we as women are going backward because we have not been as diligent and unmoving a force. We have not held a united front enough; we have not been an immovable force to be reckoned with. We have let our guard down and this cannot happen if we are to be recognized as being equal humans. Look around at the degradation of society that continues to happen and you will see the continued degradation of women.

I will move on from this chapter having just begun my rants about the inequality of women. I share these thoughts with you because I believe that the way our society is set up, the ways in which women are devalued as citizens and as people lead to the collective feeling that women are second class citizens and that it is ok to treat them as such. If it is ok to treat women as second class and of less value then it must be ok to objectify them, tell them what to do, treat them as if they are stupid, put them down and then by extension bring this type of treatment into a lot of the homes and offices that women exist in. It must be ok for men to verbally abuse and then as this progresses turning into physical abuse, it must be ok right?

In the media, in our society the outward message from domestic abuse advocates say it is never ok to raise a fist to your partner, your children. We raise our eyebrows at this obvious sign of abuse. After all, there are bruises to be seen. Broken bones, restraining orders. It is my belief that domestic violence numbers will continue to go up and up especially in the 21st century. The reasons are the old fashioned ideas that men are in charge, they have all of the rights and you as a female have fewer rights, less of an identity. Even though we are told verbally that women have progressed, things have changed and even though the dialogue about women is that we of course are "Equal" what we are SHOWN everywhere we turn is the exact opposite message which is simultaneously being told and this is the much louder message in today's society.

The next time you are in a conversation with two or more men pay attention to the dynamic between you and watch what happens to the conversation. Do you all of a sudden have no voice? Does the conversation end up being between the men who talk louder and louder above you finally leaving you out altogether? Is your voice less important than the exchange that goes on between men? Do the men forget their manners altogether because they are now in a conversation with each other? Are you now the observer of the exchange no longer able to offer your perspective or voice because no one is listening and to be heard you must contemplate shouting above them or listening quietly as any attempt to say a word is now futile?

I find this an interesting dynamic as well as a frustrating one. I have learned to speak up over the years, but if you pay attention to how the world still works you will see what I am talking about. It is subtle sometimes, but it happens with amazing regularity. If you are talking to a man and another man walks up watch and see what happens. Watch how the exchange moves and changes. Watch to see who the man attends to with his posture, his eyes and his conversation. This is an ancient behavior and few men have progressed beyond this knee jerk behavior. It is such an ingrained subconscious thing and is taught from generation to generation that I doubt many realize how much they cut women off, subtly leave them out and slowly shift focus until they are ignoring the woman they were just talking to. Luckily this is not always the case – there are many men out there who do have manners so, please forgive the generalization if you are one of those men.

To be fair I must also mention that women also do this to each other. I think that many women may have been taught as children to pay attention to their fathers and that what he says is most important. At least in the past. So in social situations when a man walks up to two women in conversation, the exchange many times will end up with the women competing for the floor and giving control over any exchange to the man. Oh the dynamics of social exchanges. Life is complicated.

Awareness by all of us in social exchanges is the key to making changes happen. In my own home with three men, my husband and my two sons, I called attention to this dynamic and it did begin to change. They were not even aware that they were involved in this way with one another. When awareness seeped in, they saw themselves and actively work on changing the behavior.

Chapter Three
The Takeover

The takeover of me. How did this happen? It happened slowly and gradually over time. The nice man I had moved in with must have started to believe that I was his property, and that he had the right and obligation to tell me what to do. The ways he tried to control me over time was in attacking me verbally about something he did not like. For example, if I was busy working I would leave a stack of papers on the floor by the couch for later reading. He would ask about it and then proceed to belittle me. He would say things like "this must be left over from your having come from South Sacramento." What he meant was I came from a lower class part of town and I was inadequate in some way because of it.

Sam acted as if when he came into my life he saved me from my South Sac existence. He always insinuated in these offhand comments that he was better than I was in some way. While I would start to defend or explain myself about this perceived inadequacy, (leaving a stack of papers next to the couch) he would change the subject and start to talk about something else he did not like. He would criticize anything and everything depending on what suited him at that moment.

I can remember, standing in the dining room defending one thing, hearing the next thing, starting to defend that, having him start criticizing a third thing. I could see him change from one subject to the next and see myself responding and feeling a sense of loss of control over anything. The conversation had veered off course. The result when it was over I would feel off balance, confused by the attack and depressed because I was not good enough somehow. Sam had succeeded in making me feel less than. He had won. If I would explain for too long, defending myself he would say "you always have to have the last word." This was a statement he was to use many times over the years as he would walk away dismissing me. I am sure he felt great satisfaction from watching me dance.

Ways in which a partner can try to control you which are:

1. **Belittling** You

2. A **putdown disguised** as a joke

3. **Sarcasm**

4. **Finding Fault**

5. Holding out a **carrot** (reward) for acceptable

behavior and then when you achieve the behavior the

carrot is moved farther out – you can never achieve it.

6. **Withholding** the very thing that he has figured out is most important to you. If it is acceptance, it is withheld, if it is sex, it is withheld, whatever your partner has figured out is the most important in terms of what he can give you in the relationship to make you happy – he will withhold it … forever.

7. Giving you **scraps** little tiny pieces of what you need to survive the marriage. Like a person dying of thirst or hunger, he will provide just enough to keep you alive and in the relationship.

8. **Deliberately going round and round in circles.**

 Deliberate confusional tactics - Denial and countering behavior - He will tell you what you heard him say, he never said. Telling you what he did and you know he did, he did not do. **You are not crazy** it just feels like it.

Belittling is the one mentioned earlier with an example. To expand on it just a bit, if you are put down in any way or if you are spoken to in a condescending tone with words that also are condescending this is part of belittling. Another is patronizing behavior. When someone speaks to you as if you are stupid with a tone and words to match this tone. You are being belittled. If someone speaks to you making comments that are designed to make you feel stupid, to say things to you that make you feel like less of a human being in your own eyes then you are being belittled.

Belittling was one of the main ways Sam used to control me. To him it was like a game. One of his ways to hurt me with words in this category was to say something about my parenting skills. If he would point out one thing that he knew I felt insecure about it would be about whether or not I was a good mom. What was confusing about this form of verbal abuse was I never expected the comments and small attacks on my security and self-esteem. This was a man who said he loved me. Why then did I feel so unloved? He typically never said anything like this at work. As a matter of fact, he ONLY said these things when we were home and when he was certain there would be NO WITNESSES.

Unfortunately my small son could be just around the corner listening sometimes. I did not know he was there until years later. If your friends, partners or mates ever do this behavior and if they do this when there is NO ONE ELSE AROUND TO HEAR IT pay attention. This is a standard mode of operation to a verbal abuser. He will only put you down when you are alone.

Putdowns disguised as a joke are one of the forms of verbal abuse you may be the most familiar with just by having lived in our society. On television, in sit coms in particular, you will hear generalizations being made about women that are intended to be a joke and are supposed to be funny. It seems that all of the old jokes have made their way into the 21st century never having gathered dust. If this bother's you of course you can always change the channel or turn off the TV. If this happens to you at home, run! Just joking. Hard to do when you have a life, family and business with the man who says these things.

Here are some examples: Women are not as smart as men. Women talk too much. Women are too sensitive. Women cry too easily. Once a month women aren't worth much. When women are pregnant we are shown to be basket cases. You are a woman, what do you know? You must be a dumb blonde. I was just kidding. Can't you take a joke? You used to think I was funny. You used to laugh at my jokes. Can't you just shut up? Oh – that's right – you're a woman. Don't' be such a whuss. You're a pussy (to other men) What's wrong with you, do you have PMS? Of course there are a million more but you definitely know what I am talking about. These are obvious statements and stereotypes that exist daily in the lives of every female. At home there are a million ways a man can use generalized statements and incorporate them into a joke that is a putdown. Some men think they are clever enough to do this type of putdown in groups and in front of others. What they think makes it ok are the words spoken right after the put down, "I was just kidding." Once again these types of jokes and putdowns disguised as jokes can become tiring and boring, but make no mistake, over time if this type of messaging is being told to you enough it will undermine your well-being. Especially in combination with #1-8 mentioned of these behaviors.

Sarcasm can be combined with the entire previous paragraph about putdowns that are disguised as a joke. Sarcastic remarks are designed to elicit a response from you or to make you defend yourself about something. As an example, "Oh that's right you are supposed to be more introspective because you are a girl" Backhanded comments that include some kind of reverse insult are sarcastic. A mocking, often ironic or satirical remark, usually intended to wound as well as amuse. A sharply ironical taunt; sneering or cutting remark.

My Sam was witty and funny in front of friends. He was a master of sarcasm at home. This was an indirect way he would cut, taunt or sneer at me with amazing regularity. Being a champion of sarcasm is not a quality to be admired especially if you are the target of the sarcastic remarks. If your mate is sarcastic at your expense and then tries to laugh the remarks off as jokes, you may want to rethink being involved with such a mate.

Finding Fault – In this category the verbal abuser tries to make sure that nothing is his (their) fault. He (they) is/are an expert at gathering up all of the fault in every situation that will occur in a partnership or marriage and bring it all to you to be laid at your feet with much forethought and deliberation. If your mate can make sure that everything is your fault he (they) does/do not have to take responsibility for anything. Anything that goes wrong I might add. If things go well or are right, then of course he had everything to do with those things – but remember he has nothing to do with anything that goes wrong. When that happens everything is YOUR FAULT. This is also called placing blame. If you are to blame for anything or everything that goes wrong in this relationship, he gets off scott free. In my case, after Sam and I split up he could walk away feeling that he was not to blame for anything and he could be the good guy in his own eyes. In his own eyes the failure of our relationship was all my fault and he believed he was the victim.

Carrots and rewards – controlling you by the reward system. In this situation your mate, or partner or even a friend give you messages like if you do this or that you can have (whatever you are wanting). Believe it or not, these messages can be given to you in a non-verbal way. Over time the perpetrator of this type of behavior has figured out what you want each day to make you happy and to make you want to stay in the relationship. In my case, I would try to be a good partner, making dinner every day and having it on the table, making sure I was home when he got there, making sure no toys were left in the living room for him to see and trying to take care of whatever needs Sam might have. I would try and anticipate what Sam would want and what would make him happy. Everyday. The more effort I put into this endeavor the further away he would move the carrot. For me, being all of the things I thought he wanted, a good wife, not arguing, not doing anything to upset the balance we had achieved, not asking for much was supposed to get me what I wanted.

What I wanted was kindness, affection and some form of intimacy. Once in a very great while this formula worked for me. But, mostly it worked for him because this was how he controlled my behavior and me. I used to run home at night in a hurry telling my son, "Hurry, daddy is waiting." I never wanted my son to upset my husband because then I would not get the carrot, I would not be rewarded for good behavior. My son's behavior could make or break my reward. And, sometimes my punishment.

Living this way, waiting for some scrap of attention or affection, trying to do everything right was an extension of my childhood dynamic. Walking on those eggshells. I was an expert at it, but it still did not get me what I longed for. My husband's real love and attention. I still did not realize that he could not really love anyone. He was broken and if he kept me broken I would stay. My husband lived in a different reality than mine. I would eventually learn what that meant. For the sake of an easy way to think about this just imagine speaking to Chinese to a person that only understands English. Unless one understands arm gestures or facial expressions it will be difficult to understand the meaning involved in such an exchange. It was very much like this in my home. Asking myself how did this happen as I would walk away. I was always trying for understanding and we were not speaking the same language.

Before you say out loud boo hoo, you were so stupid to stay, why didn't you just leave? Remember, this happened over the course of 10 plus years. I was almost thirteen years younger than this man. I thought I had married the kind, caring charismatic version of him. I had bought that version of who he wanted me to see, wanted me to believe in. Once I fell for that version and had committed to being with that version, he had me.

I created a life and a business with this man; he was the father figure to my son. By the time I figured out what had happened I was well into the relationship. Quite a lot of time had gone by and was going by. I was so puzzled by our relationship I was continually in my head thinking, trying to figure out what had gone wrong and where the man I thought I had known and who I had committed myself to had gone. Slow, insidious conditioning. Keeping me off balance each day was the key to his success. The nice version of this man made appearances just often enough for me to hold out hope that I would find the key to getting this version of him back in my life. Hope kept me motivated and locked in.

Withholding – this was his favorite one. He loved them all, but this was the one he took the most enjoyment from. Yes, I said enjoyment. My mate would withhold the very thing he had discovered was most important to me. If you are female, quite a lot of us would feel that love, caring, acceptance, understanding, physical intimacy and connection would be all or among the things that would be most important in a long term commitment or partnership. If your mate has figured out that you need to be understood, **he will always act like he does not understand**. This leaves you forever explaining. If I could just figure out the right way, the right words to explain it you think, then he would finally understand me. This would make it easier to connect to him. Right? The thing is, **even if he understands whatever it is you are trying to get him to understand he will act as though he does not. He will withhold his understanding…forever.**

If he determines you want to hold hands while walking together and that this is important to you he will rarely or NEVER do it. He will withhold his hand from you. Forever... If your mate determines that you want to have quiet time to yourself, a certain amount of time every day or every week, he won't let you have it. He will interrupt or find other things for you to do. Even if it is to fight with him. He will NEVER allow you to have the quiet time you have expressed you need. **He will do his best to make sure you never get what you want...Forever.... Don't fool yourself into believing this will ever change. Once your mate has the formula down it will continue... forever...**

Scraps – This is how I survived for so long in this relationship. Every once in a while so that I wouldn't leave or give up on this relationship Sam would actually sit down and talk to me. He would listen to my concerns and promise to do better. I would be hopeful. He would give me these scraps of attention and pretend to give me what I wanted by saying he would try harder to provide what I was asking. This was only lip service. He would be nice for a week and then go back to his normal version of how can we get Laurie to jump through hoops?

The thing that kept me going for so long is that my livelihood was intertwined with this man. Our business was how we made a living together, we had a good working relationship. As long as we were friends this worked. We were friends and business partners at work. We ran our company together for years. This part of the dynamic worked. He was smart and had vision. He was great at making money until he wasn't. Our business relationship was the better part of the relationship. It worked well. The rest of it from dinnertime on sucked. I asked for more commitment, more attention, more affection, more time, throughout our relationship. These were the things he did not want to give and could not give. He sidestepped me; put me off for a very long time.

If I wanted to connect with him in a physical way, he would say he was tired and I should see him in the morning. In the morning he would be up and be gone early. I admit I quit trying. I stopped mentioning it, because if I did mention it, he would withhold it. Physical connection had to be his idea and it rarely was. He did not want to be vulnerable and connected to me. If he ever was it would be too dangerous to his whole way of living. If he was ever vulnerable and really connected to me he would lose his power. This was also part of the Withholding plan he subscribed to.

I can only think that this must have been the way his father treated his mother. This was what he learned about how relationships worked. At the end, I remember calling Sam's sister asking her at last, "What happened to Sam when you were growing up?" "Did something traumatic happen to him that you can share with me?" Sam's sister could think of nothing or at least nothing she would or could share with me. He was so shut down that once when he had to have surgery and almost died, for just one moment I saw a vulnerable side to him.

Sam had surgery to remove part of his colon. He was in the hospital for 16 days. During that time at first I was terrified, wondering how can I do this alone? I was also angry because I had told him to go to the Doctor. He did not. So, when he began to complain about pain and discomfort I once again told him to go to the Doctor. He did not. That week a few days before his intestines blew up; he went out gambling and drinking. So I thought well, he couldn't be that sick. This was a Wednesday right before the Fourth of July weekend. On the morning of the 4th he woke up in pain, and could not stand up straight. He said he thought he needed to go to the hospital. Remember – he made me think he wasn't really that sick. I was angry because he never went to the Doctor and never told me how bad it was.

While Sam was in the hospital I realized that I already did everything for our business, our home and our child. The only thing I did not do was take out the garbage and mow the lawn. I realized for the first time that over time I had become the person who did most of the work in running our business and home. I also did most of the work in our relationship. Sam had plenty of time to play golf, hang out with friends and do things without me.

When Sam came home from the hospital, for about a week he was vulnerable and I saw a part of this man I had seen early in our relationship. He said to me "I don't know if I know how to love. I can't feel it; I think I only feel the edges of it." For a brief moment I had hope. He would cry too because he almost died, he felt he had no power, no control.

One evening while sitting at the dinner table alone Sam asked me about a hamster I had bought our son while he was in the hospital. He did not like the idea of having a hamster because who would end up cleaning the cage? It turned out that what really made him mad about this purchase was that **I did not have his permission or his consent to buy the hamster.** He overreacted in his anger and reached over and slapped me across the face for doing this without his permission. I was in shock! Gone were my hopes, gone was the man who had felt something for a moment. The man who had power and control over all of us was back. His anger, his slap helped him feel in control and making me feel bad gave him back his power.

Crazy making and denial – this behavior has to do with denying what was said or done in any exchange. For example, if I say what do you want for dinner and you say I would like chicken. I go and cook chicken and you say I didn't want chicken, I say yes you did, that's what you said you wanted. You say no I never said that. If done over time, his denial that he said what you heard and what you know he said is called crazy making behavior. He can deny anything that happens in your relationship or marriage or partnership. This includes the fact that what he says is abusive and eventually what he does, like slapping your face never happened.

Once Sam had been out having a few beers. When he returned I complained about his being out until 3:00 a.m. I had made dinner and he did not show up. He had not called. We argued and were in the middle of a heated exchange in the kitchen. The next thing I knew he took what he had in his hand at the time (it was a hardboiled egg) and bashed it into my chest crushing it. He knocked me off balance because what he did was so unexpected. I fell over on to the floor and he knelt next to me. Next, he had my chin in his hand. I think he was trying to keep me from saying anything more so he pushed on my chin upward, he did this so hard that I began to think he would break my neck and I let out a muffled scream. At this point he stopped.

When I tried to talk to him about it in a day or two, wanting to clear the air, talk it out because it had scared me so badly, he said "you don't know what you are talking about, that never happened. You are a liar." This is denial and is designed to make you crazy. If your partner can minimize what he has done or deny that he ever did it whether it is verbal or physical you are experiencing crazy making behavior. This can be very dangerous territory because if you are being physically hurt and your partner is denying it things can escalate quickly to assault and battery. He may even believe you are lying. That way he can ignore his own behavior.

Who knows how many beers Sam actually had that night. That may explain his lack of memory when it came to this incident. The other part of this equation is that when someone drinks or does drugs it is never a good time to complain about it or confront them. You can get hurt, verbally and physically. It does not pay to try to talk to someone who is high. This is also a reason they may not remember the abuse. This is also a way to minimize it and deny it ever happened. This can be dangerous.

Something interesting I learned along the way about people who abuse alcohol. It explains a lot about some of the "missing" memories of abuse. What I learned is the fact that if a person learns to do a new task while they are high and then tries to complete the same task sober, most of the time they cannot do the task sober. They have no real memory of having learned the task. But! If they try to do the task again when they are drunk, they remember how to and can complete it. If your partner drinks too much or if they do drugs, in addition to already having abusive personality traits when you combine the two life can become very confusing and can be very dangerous to you.

In my case Sam was very good at masking the amount of alcohol he was consuming. I did not recognize for quite some time that I was not talking to a sober person. Some people can drink quite a lot and still function (or seem to be doing fine) and it can be hard to decipher or tell if they are themselves or not. He would drive home and get there in one piece. I was so not seeing what I should have seen, should have known. Denial worked for quite some time. Don't let this be you.

The lists and information you have just read are what I personally call the behaviors of a Narcissist and these were the things that I personally experienced. There are many sites and many lists about verbal abuse on the internet. One of the terms I personally don't like is "Gaslighting" which was taken from an old film. Gaslighting is what I called crazy making and denial on the previous pages.

Gaslighting describes actions that 1) make another person believe he or she is crazy, and 2) discredit the person by making others think they are crazy. The term comes from the play and 1944 movie **_Gaslight_** starring Charles Boyer and Ingrid Bergman. In this movie, the Charles Boyer character, acts as a primary aggressor. What he does is to manipulate the gas light in the house randomly from the attic. When the Ingrid Bergman character, his wife, reports this, he responds as though her perception is wrong. Because she has no explanation and because his manner is confident, she begins to doubt herself. It is not necessary to deliberately manipulate the environment to gaslight another person (although this happens).

Here is a list that is simple:

Being called names, he uses words to shame, Yelling, swearing and screaming, Using threats to intimidate, Blaming the victim, Your feelings are dismissed, you often wonder why you feel so bad, and lastly, Manipulating your actions. I have listed this source in my bibliography. This source also explains how to respond to abuse.

Chapter Four

Other Warning Signs/RED FLAGS

In the beginning of our friendship and relationship Sam gave the impression, a very good impression that he liked everyone, he would nurture their talents at work. He presented the illusion of a man who was happy bringing all of these various talents among his subordinates together making a good, cohesive and complimentary family environment in which to work and live. He knew how to make people feel a part of something and that we were on the same team.

Everyone seemed to like him and he was "The Boss" at work. He had risen to a key position within a large computer company in the late 70's being in charge of the entire Western Region and all by the time he was 33. I did not find out until a long time later that he would manipulate and play us against one another to try to get more from each of us. In conversations about other people I began to notice his superior attitude. Unfortunately for me this was way into the relationship.

When he would talk to me about people who had more education than he did, he would say it didn't matter. He would say, "Those who cannot do teach." Or he would talk about being street smart. People who had Bachelor's degrees were a great target. Especially those who held marketing degrees and public relations degrees. He would say, "Look at them, they work for someone else." "They don't have what it takes to run their own company." Picture that being said in a snide way or with a sneer.

Truth be told, he was jealous of them, the many people out there who did have an education. He even lied to his friends, telling them he had graduated from Marquette University. This was a man who only had a high school education and who had read the one-minute salesman. Once in a while he had gone to a sales training course. He was right he was street smart and he did have a knack, a talent. He was a success for a while.

He always looked down on others and always put down other people verbally. His jokes were almost always about putting others down. "They" were not as good as he was so he could be the good guy in his own eyes. The only trouble was that his self-esteem was so low this was the only way he could make himself feel better.

This is a man who could cut anyone to the quick in a sentence or at most a paragraph. Especially me. I recall vividly and so does my son of being in Marie Calendars' one evening for dinner on the way home from some event. Sam verbally put down our waitress so much so that I was extremely embarrassed and I tried to intervene, tried to make light of what he was saying as though it was a joke or anything but what it was. It was humiliating for our server and me. I wanted to save her from it but could not. This is something Sam would do whenever he felt like it and he did not mind doing this in front of our son.

Here are a few warning signs in addition to the ones mentioned previously.
If your partner criticizes people… a lot… almost every day or everyday

If you feel tense on edge around him (not in a good way) why do you think this is?

If you don't feel like you can relax and be yourself
Are you worried he will criticize you or does he already do that?

Does he seem interested in what you have to say?
Does he criticize your family?
Does he criticize your friends?
When you are on the phone with ANYONE does he hover near by?

Does he ask who are you talking to and what are you talking about?

When you get off the phone with whomever you were talking to does he criticize them? He is trying to control you by getting you to feel negatively about your friends, your family and anyone else who would take time and attention away from him?

If you express an interest in taking a class or taking dance or skydiving – it doesn't matter what the activity is – just doing something you might enjoy does he try to discourage you from doing them by expressing negative concerns about what might happen if you do those things? Or his tactic could be that by criticizing the activity, belittling it or you for wanting to try it he is trying to control you. If he can keep you isolated from others, you are easier to control.

Does your partner have a separate life from you (does he hang out with his friends a lot?) Does he tell you what HE is going to do rather than discussing things together?

Some of the examples I give of what happened to me may seem obvious to anyone who might be reading this. Sometimes the way someone treats you is so over the top wrong and can be so obvious you may wonder what it is that I am using so many words to tell you. When I say in the title of this book uncomfortably numb I am telling you how this type of relationship and this type of treatment over time is a very subtle numbing of a person. The numbing of your experience and feelings as you try to overlook how you are treated on a daily basis is what happens. Slowly over time you begin questioning everything about yourself. You begin to think there must be something wrong with you.

The reason you think it may be you might possibly have to do with how you were treated as a child or how you mistakenly think relationships work. If you were ignored, discounted, treated as though you were not important by original family members you have a long history and experience with thinking this type of treatment is normal. I am repeating this because it is important in recognizing what is happening or may have happened to you.

The verbal abuser in my life treated me in a decent fashion just enough in our relationship for me to have hope of change, hope of his understanding, hope of a real connection. I had thought we had really connected in the beginning of our relationship and I felt so attached and in love with this man from that connection I hung in there for a very long time trying to catch a glimpse of the man I thought I knew. I wondered where he had gone and what was I doing that did not seem to bring that out in him. I had taken responsibility for the change thinking that somehow it was my fault.

If you overlook disrespect and unkind words they will continue to come. In order to change the dynamic, you have to be willing to say "I don't deserve to be spoken to like that." You need to say "Stop it" Do not engage in this type of exchange. If necessary, you must walk away. Do not play with him verbally. What I mean is do not engage in verbal sparring. When I was attacked verbally, especially when I was completely caught off guard I would try to explain, defend, make him understand. This was an impossible task leaving me feeling battered and bruised emotionally. There was never any understanding and no conflict was ever really resolved. I would have to wait until the next morning to start with a clean slate and try not to get in trouble again.

I knew our relationship had veered off course from the very beginning. I could not understand what had happened to cause this to occur. I had committed myself to this relationship and so I hung in there thinking if I could just unlock the mystery to how this had happened and thinking also that I knew how to make a good relationship work, I would have a wonderful one with Sam after all. I could somehow bring this man along with me, sort of like the fantasy where I show him how good it could be, if only he would just open his eyes and see I would show it to him.

Eventually I realized and even said to him, I am not to blame for your anger, you were angry long before I met you. You brought all of this with you into our relationship. I realized over time that this man had treated his ex-wife the same way and that this was all he knew how to do. He was broken and so was I. But, until I could discover this simple truth and begin to change our dynamic I was to suffer every day trying to find the key to unlocking the nice version of the man I had thought I met and thought I had known.

This was a very addictive relationship. I was hooked into it from the beginning. I was friends with this man first and liked him. He was clever, smart, and funny. He was a savvy business person. I wanted to learn how to create a successful life and business. I thought this was the guy to show me and this was the guy to do it with. I believed that ultimately I would have everything I had wanted and hoped for. I was extremely wrong.

I knew that a person could be addicted to substances or gambling or other vices. Sometimes the answer to the question why did she stay is about addiction to the relationship. My mother used to say "It's like banging your head against a stone wall, it feels so good when you quit." How can one be addicted to a relationship or to a dynamic that is bad for you? This is the addictive relationship. Part of the abusive relationship that appears to work is the two partners' addiction to it.

The abuser is always struggling with his need to feel in control and needs his partner as a means to that end. The partner needs to feel connected and understood. She continually strives for connection with her abuser and the feeling that her partner understands her. The abuser is in a wrestling match with himself (and with his partner) to stay on top, to feel power and control over his spouse or partner and his family. He needs to maintain that feeling no matter the cost to his partner or the relationship. It is all that he knows and most likely he is completely unaware of his motivation. Even if he is aware his behaviors are working for him and he likely enjoys it.

She is in a struggle to try and gain a partnership that eludes her, connection and understanding that also eludes her. She thinks she can fix it (herself, him and the relationship) she is willing to put all of her effort into gaining these things from or with her partner every day. Every day she uses all of her understanding, thoughts, feelings and efforts struggling and wrestling with herself and him to at last finally achieve acceptance, love and to have her partner care about her in a real way. The problem with this is that each person has completely separate goals and agendas. These are two separate worlds they exist in. The abuser cannot and will not connect because if he does he loses power and control. No matter what the partner does to achieve closeness and connection he cannot allow it.

"If Only" thinking is a part of the addiction. She keeps thinking, if only I could make him understand who and what I am. If only he could understand how much he means to me he would "get it" and return my love. If only he would talk to me. If only he would return to being the man I met (where did he go?) If only I can find the key to this mystery, we can fix our relationship. The understanding will never come; the "real" connection will never come. This is how and why the relationship continues and the power struggle continues. Neither person wants to say "Uncle." This wrestling match goes on for years because each party is trying to sort of "win the argument."

In my case I wanted to open his eyes. Show him the way out of what had happened to what I thought was once our good relationship. I was deluding myself because the good relationship had never existed. It was an illusion sold to me by my partner to suck me into the relationship. Once sold, I was in it. I fell in love with a man and a relationship that was not real and did not exist. Once I finally really got it there was no return to my delusional thinking.

The addictive part for both partners in an abusive relationship is what ultimately keeps couples together. She is confused and wants the guy she had met back in her life. If she realizes he never existed and that part of the manipulation on his part was to get her to believe he really is or was a nice guy then she will try, and try, and try to regain that relationship. Wow, what a waste of time that is/was. I used to grieve at least ten years of lost time in my life. This is why battered women stay and why the men continue to fight for power and control by showing her who is boss. She wants to fix it and he wants to control it. Do you see any winners here?

Chapter 5
The conditioning of women

I have mentioned a couple of times that we as humans are conditioned in our original family by teachers, society, and the many messages we receive every day. If you were lucky enough to be raised by a family that did not unintentionally or intentionally condition you to feel as though you were less than a brother, or a father, or remind you that by societies standards by virtue of the fact that you do not have the same body parts as a boy/man that you are already seen as unequal then you are among a very lucky group. Whew!

I am aware that there are strong women out there who have had wonderful fathers, brothers, and mothers and so on. I am aware that happy, well adjusted, smart, kind and loving families exist. I have a few friends I have talked with about this dynamic and I know that these women never felt discounted or less than in their original families.

My experience is and was more in tune with being treated differently because I was "just a girl." It's funny how a phrase becomes part of minimizing who and what you are in some people's eyes. It took me a while to realize that as an adult woman my mother has in fact become my friend. We do have quite a bit in common. One of the phrases we have used in my family over the entire length of my life when calling on the telephone in particular and upon leaving a message is "It's just me, It's just your mom." A few years ago I told my mom that I think maybe we should take out the phrase "It's Just" because I think it minimizes us. She agreed.   My brother still says" it's just your brother" when he calls.

Who knows exactly where it started but I might suggest that for she and I as female people it may have begun as what my mom wrote in her poem called "Just a Girl." My mother's childhood was in the 1940's so you can see what the thinking was at the time. When she sent me a copy I realized that this was what she carried into my childhood and my upbringing because this was what she experienced and what she knew. Patterns handed down from generation to generation.

Just a Girl by Anita McHale Price (2006)

When I was little
And just a girl
Boys' games were not forbidden
Just frowned upon
For little ladies

To throw and hit
And jump and run
Was really just so gauche
Ladies were too sweet and tidy
To slide to second base

When I was little
And just a girl
My feet were faster
Than any boy I knew
They chased me home from school
To steal a little kiss
But couldn't ever catch me

When I was little
And Just a girl
I could climb a tree
And go much higher
Than any boy I knew

They were all afraid
When branches bent and cracked
They'd crash to earth and
Break their little neck
I had no fear of falling

I knew that I could fly
Then one day they clipped my wings
With very little effort
Just two small words were all it took
To ground me for a lifetime

In a heartbeat I became
That sweet and tidy little lady
And said goodbye forever more
To the strongest part of me
No self-respecting daddy's girl

Could ever answer to the epithet
Hey – Tom Boy

You're just a girl

In this chapter I will talk about how some specific messages we have heard and are conditioned to believe can affect how we feel about ourselves and sometimes how we end up picking a mate that will reinforce negative thoughts about ourselves. The first message out there that comes to mind is that we as females are not as rational or logical as a man. Another is that women are more emotional which can affect our memory (making us less reliable). This image brings to mind the idea that a woman must need a man's help to do or accomplish most things. She must attach to a man in order to be whole. She needs a man to tell her what to do. Yes, it is the 21st century. Some women do continue to believe these messages. Certainly there are many men who believe them.

This way of thinking about ourselves if we believe it, make it easy to not only end up in a verbally abusive relationship, but it also makes it difficult for us to recognize this relationship for what it is. If we ourselves believe these statements about ourselves how can we not believe it when our mate says these things about us also? If we question ourselves when we really know something is not right, if we are unsure of the fact that being treated as less than is not right how can we recognize what verbal abuse is? If we wonder, why do I feel so badly after a verbal exchange with our mate, if we first think it must be our fault then there is something wrong with how we think about ourselves.

I say to you the obvious thing that precipitates change "Change your thinking, change your life." It is a simple idea for sure, but it is totally true. In a verbally abusive relationship the object of the game for the abuser is to keep your self-esteem low or to make sure it is non-existent. If you believe your partner is rational it is easy for you to believe the fault, the reason you are talked to disrespectfully, must be your own fault. What a trap this is. You can spend years trying to figure out what you have done wrong and to keep trying different ways of behaving to try and achieve the desired result which is having your mate treat you with care and respect, love and so on. This will most likely never happen.

Remember, the dynamic is about power and control. If your mate is a verbal abuser, his way of controlling you is to keep you off balance and to make sure you never really get what it is you want from the relationship. The reason is if he is ever vulnerable and really tries to connect with you in a real and authentic way he will (in his mind) lose his power and become weak in his own eyes. He has no idea how to really connect with anyone on a real level anyway. Or to clarify further he has no idea how to move into your reality of what love is and connect with you. He lives in his own reality and he has his own ideas about how relationships work. Loving each other in the way that he knows you want to is too scary a thought. Your world in his mind is where he loses power and control.

Many times Sam and I would go on short trips to get away from work. He liked to stay at nice resorts with golf courses and other amenities. One particular trip comes to mind when it comes to his irrational behavior, why he did it and my reaction to it. We had checked into our room on a beautiful day. It was warm spring weather. Sam and I decided to go out to dinner to this very lovely restaurant, taking our time to enjoy our dinner. We had nice conversation, enjoying each other's company without interruption. The kid was left with a sitter at home. We were on our own and so far so good. I was relaxed, having had wine with dinner as did he. On the way back to the resort, which was a short drive all was nice and good. We got out of the car and I was holding Sam's hand happily talking about some thing or another. He seemed to be in the same light carefree mood. I remember laughing with him about something we had talked about.

We went inside our room and started to get ready for bed. I put on a night gown that was long and satiny green. All of a sudden, just looking at me Sam's demeanor changed completely from one second to the next as though a button had been pushed. His verbal attack came from out of the blue like a slap across the face. I don't even recall the exact words he spoke; it was more the way he spoke to me. Angry, spitting words at me. Something like, "you always want to ruin everything. You always want something more." When Sam saw me in my night attire he had suddenly turned into a mean, angry man. He reached over to me and grabbing the straps of my gown pulling on them so hard ripping my night gown, tearing it beyond repair. I had no idea in that moment what had happened. I thought maybe he had too much to drink with dinner.

All I know is that I had thought we had enjoyed each other's company and we were alone, it was a possibility in my thinking that we might end the evening by being intimate. This apparently was too much closeness for Sam for one evening. His way of reacting to the possibility of actually connecting to me or actually carrying our connection into a physical one was to completely sabotage the moment and the rest of our night by being mean in one huge angry burst. This behavior was so irrational. I knew I had done nothing to warrant this treatment, but was confused by his actions. I ended up by taking my night gown off and throwing it in the garbage can.

There was no talking about this and we both knew it. I went to bed in a T-shirt feeling hopelessly hurt and depressed. This is so obvious that this was Sam's problem and not about me. Please forgive my naivety and confusion. I was old enough to understand what this was, but I was still confused by this type of behavior. Sam had been afraid of losing control by being intimate with me at the end of a great day. He had to revert back to some feeling of control by being mean to me ending any chance of connecting with me on a physical level. He felt out of control in those situations. This will completely ruin your sex life.

Obviously this was Sam's problem. I knew he felt the least amount of control in situations where he perceived there was any expectation from me. At the time, this did not help. Sam had to blame his problem on me by saying I always wanted more.

This extreme irrational behavior did not occur frequently because I think Sam must have known it would cause me to question it and examine it more closely. It would have made it too obvious that he was the one with the bigger problem. So, these extreme incidents were not as prevalent as subtler ways of sabotaging our interactions.

He never apologized for his behavior when these things happened. The next morning, we went to breakfast not mentioning the night before. I knew not to mention it, to pretend nothing was wrong that nothing had happened. We had a quiet more subdued breakfast, but I did not try to come close to him again.

The rest of our time off together was more of his making. He had succeeded in making the rest of his vacation more to his comfort and more at the distance from me that he was comfortable with. I remember he went to play golf while I stayed in the room. I sat in the Jacuzzi tub alone with my thoughts and alone with the seriousness of what my relationship really was. I was once again distracted from this thinking once I returned home to my busy life at work and raising our son. Hard to dwell on what had happened for long. I continued counseling and examining my life, my motivations and my life with Sam.

When you are conditioned to this type of behavior there is a code of silence that must be observed in order to avoid chaos on a daily basis. If irrational behavior is ignored, this is part of the unspoken contract and conditioning that goes on in an abusive relationship. If you are told that you are too sensitive, you always ruin things, ask for too much, you are always trying to be right, you are illogical and you don't make sense, these are all statements designed to condition you, to make you believe that interactions gone wrong are your fault.

What happens over time is you lower your expectations about what you want and deserve from this relationship. Slowly you begin to give up when it comes to asking for more, asking for change, and trying to talk to your mate. Eventually you realize that this endeavor is hopeless. I knew that I had to somehow leave this situation when I had the thoughts, how do I survive this relationship? And then the thought, how can I outlive this man? I had promised to take care of him when he was old. I had promised. I thought I was going to end up just waiting for this man to die in order to be free. That was when I realized "what in the heck are you thinking?" "Do you hear what you just said to yourself?" This is the moment I knew I had to find my way out while I was still alive. This is when I was certain that this was the time to get out and get a divorce. In my case, there was to be no happy ending to this. I had hoped for it all along. I had wanted to bring my partner with me into the light. It was never going to happen. I was eventually going to have to save myself, walk into the light without him and start over once again.

Chapter 6
More definable qualities of verbal abuse

Every verbal abuser is different and each has individual ways of saying things that are designed to cut you to the quick and make sure you know that he or she is in control. I have shared some of the specific things I have dealt with. My verbal abuser used almost all of the things I will list in this chapter. In Chapter Three I mentioned several types of abuse. Unfortunately, there are more to choose from and more to indulge in if you are the abuser.

If your partner, friend or spouse has some of these qualities consistently you may want to see a counselor with your partner or even go without him. This can help you learn better what you are dealing with. For example, is your partner angry frequently for no reason you can fathom?

Is he irritable, intense, does he pout about things and not express anything? Does he try to control who you are friends with and have relationships with including or especially your family? Is he critical a lot? Is he really good at putting people down directly and indirectly (using jokes indirectly)? Is his temper explosive and is he hostile? Is he a different man in public? Is he a nice guy, charming and charismatic in public? Is his personality basically different in public versus at home making you think he is a Dr. Jeckel Mr. Hyde type of guy?   Does he try to manipulate your behavior by using words to make you work harder at anything you do like keeping the house or making sure his life is comfortable? Does he try to get you to do more of anything or everything to take care of the household or work you started out sharing?

Is most of it now your responsibility while he has less and less responsibility to your home and relationship?   Are you doing all the work in the relationship giving 110% to 150% while he barely puts anything into it? I call this my visual seesaw. If you are holding down one end while he is up in the air enjoying the sights from up there while you do all the work – what is happening in this relationship? Everything seems out of balance because it is out of balance.

Did he change almost overnight once you were married? (Or began living with him)?   Is he jealous frequently about nothing? Does it seem like you are in a competition with him and that he is always the winner? No matter what you say in conversation with him does he take the opposite view point on everything and try to tell you you are wrong? For example, today I say the sky is so blue and he argues that it isn't. Tomorrow, the sky is the same shade of blue as yesterday and I say gee the sky is a dark shade of blue today and he argues, no it isn't it is the same shade as yesterday, just blue. I hope that makes sense to you. My relationship was one where he had to be right and I had to be wrong.

My abuser said when he met me that he believed women were of equal value, they should be paid equally for the same jobs and he seemed to have a progressive point of view. He seemed to be a male supporter of feminism. This exact opposite turned out to be true. It was probably more of a challenge and more fun for him to break my spirit because I am a feminist and these are the things I believe. He did once say to me "I liked you better before you became liberated." The thing is I was "liberated" before I knew him. He sought to change that and he sought to conquer that. He almost did.

Examples follow of uncommunicative behaviors. There were many times when I would speak to Sam and I would wait for a response looking at him and waiting. Sam would not blink, nod, or move in any way to show that he had heard me. It was as if I had not spoken at all. I was for all intents and purposes invisible. He would not acknowledge me in any way. I would ask him a direct question and I would frequently get the same non-response. Sometimes I would say "Did you hear me?" He would again not respond until a very, very long pause had occurred and then he would finally answer saying "Yes I heard you." His way of doing this, his motivation was to remind me that in all ways, including conversation, he was in charge and in control. He was in charge of whether we would even have a conversation.

Invariably he would then say, "Why do I have to answer right away, maybe I am thinking about it?" "I should be able to think about what I want to say before I talk." Trouble is – most of the time I could not even get that much from him. If he wanted to talk about anything I was to be there to listen and be allowed to interject on occasion. If I instigated the discussion I was frequently met with a blank, brick wall.

Sometimes though he was nice and we could talk to each other especially about work. Other times and I never knew when or why it changed I was met with nothing. What was confusing about this was the way he was at work and in front of others. He was that charming guy I mentioned. In our business relationships we did a lot of networking going to mixers and business related events. In these situations, I began to notice if I would leave the room to go to the ladies' room for example, I would come back to the group he was standing with and frequently he would not move an inch to include me in the space next to him in the group. Sometimes he would even keep his back to me and not acknowledge my presence. It was very subtle. Once I asked him, did you notice you do this? He of course said no he did not realize he did this. He said he would try to do better.

One of Sam's favorite things to do would be the exact opposite of what I would ask him to do. Example: Sam knew I was a little nervous in the car so when we would leave to go down a windy curvy mountain road on our way to visit family he would drive. Sometimes on certain curves or on certain areas of road I would get more uncomfortable with the speed we would come down the mountain so I would ask him if he would please slow down a little. These were also times when he would not answer me. His response to me would be to speed up and scare me even more. He would do it to the point of my saying please, please slow down. He would ignore me until he was good and ready to slow down. I think he really enjoyed this. I made mental notes to not ask him to slow down. Over time this man learned what my fears or insecurities were and then took advantage of those things to make me squirm.

Example: If we had been to a visit with my father and stepmom especially if I had a good feeling about the visit, if I seemed happy or content with the way things had gone Sam would pick apart and dissect everyone's behavior. Finding fault with each person we had just seen. He would criticize and break down what he thought each person's motivations were and talked about what he perceived as their shortcomings. He would talk about how he thought they should have behaved. He would complain about the gifts received at Christmas. I remember saying to him after he started in one time, "I just had a nice visit, and can't you please let me have that for just a little while?"

One trip we made very late in our relationship, (towards the end of it) when our young son was about

4 was a trip together to the Santa Cruz Boardwalk. Not long after we arrived as we were in line to pay for our tickets for the day I told Sam I needed to use the restroom. I pointed to where the restrooms were and said I would be right back. I never take long in the bathroom as it is one of my least favorite places to be. I literally walked fast to and from the bathroom and did indeed come right back.

Sam and my small son were nowhere to be seen. I thought well that's odd. They should be nearby since I was not gone long. I showed Sam where the bathroom was. So I stood looking around and told myself to be patient and calm as they probably went to the men's room or something. I waited and wondered. Then I asked a guy in a booth if he had seen them. He had not. I tried to joke and make light of their disappearance thinking "don't panic I am sure there is a reasonable explanation." After about twenty minutes of this I started to walk a bit faster looking around. I thought if I stayed in one place (where I left them) they would show up. They did not. So I began to look. I called into the men's room asking a guy if they were in there. I started to look down the Boardwalk and walked faster looking for them. Then I began to panic as the thought occurred to me, what if Sam lost track of our son and he was frantically looking for him? Then panic set in because I thought about how fast a small child can disappear. I was getting scared now.

I was moving farther and faster down the Boardwalk far away from the ticket booth and the bathroom I had been in for 2 minutes or less. Where were they???? Just at the point when I could stand it no longer and truly began to panic even more I finally saw them coming toward me from the opposite end of the Boardwalk, with our son on Sam's shoulders. I of course being in panic mode was like "where in the heck were you?" "Where did you go and why? I came right back why did you leave?" All Sam did was laugh at me and then get annoyed because I had been so scared. He thought it was funny. I suspected he had done this on purpose. He most likely had. This way, he looked rational, I looked irrational and it was a crappy start to our day (for me).

His explanation was that he had gone looking for me at the bathroom. I said why would I have gone to the other end of the board walk without the two of you? It was completely illogical to have done so. I had pointed to the bathroom just feet away from the ticket booth. None of this made any sense to me whatsoever. But, Sam thought it was funny to scare me like that and it did not bother him in the slightest that he had been missing with our small boy for more than half an hour. I was puzzled at his behavior except to say that he seemed to get a kick out of my reaction to his disappearance with our small boy. This is how crazy my life had become. It seemed Sam would try to find ways to manipulate me into looking like I was the irrational one and he seemed to relish being able to increase my stress level or ruin my day if at all possible.

Over time I began to really see patterns of disengagement. I learned that one of the ways Sam could keep from getting too attached or too involved with me was to make sure he did not look at me directly. It was sort of a glance in my direction almost out of his peripheral vision. If I was just a blurry image somewhere over to one side, if Sam never actually looked at my face, in my eyes he could much better keep me at arm's length and at a comfortable distance. For him. One of the most basic things needed for connection (eye contact) was denied. I eventually got to the point where I was not only defending myself from verbal attacks but the dance I was doing also included positioning myself (or trying to) directly in front of him so that he would have to see me. I did this once in the kitchen when he was on one of his tirades and with my feet and face squarely in front of him I said "Wake Up, Wake Up! If you keep doing this, you will end up alone." Then I walked away.

I have to include an example of another woman's experience and how she fell into this type of relationship. This is a common occurrence and one can find these stories all over the internet currently. I was not so lucky because these things happened in my world before there was an internet. Here is the story for many a loving female she said:

"I fell hard and fast. Overwhelmed by his attention and adoration, I jumped in headfirst without blinking, believing him after only weeks of dating when he declared his never-ending love and that I was his soul mate, that I had brought meaning into his meaningless existence." The categories mentioned are things to keep an eye open for.

Love Bombing

A manipulation tactic involving lavish demonstrations and constant bombardments of attention and affection is an attempt to gain control by moving the relationship forward quickly. Everything he did was perfect. Everything he said was perfect. As if he had some insight into my soul and what I wanted in a relationship. This was before I knew anything about "Grooming."

Grooming – A calculated and predatory act of maneuvering a person into a more dependent and isolated position by claiming a "special connection" where they are more vulnerable to accepting future abusive behavior. "I gave him everything without question, without reservation: my kindness, my loyalty, my love, my forgiveness (over and over again) But that was before I knew about just how Empathic I was.

Empathic - A highly sensitive and empathic person who feels and often takes on the emotions of others often at the expense of their own emotional well-being.

This is a female characteristic used against a woman by the abuser.

Pathological Liar (This could be an abusers MO) A person who habitually and compulsively lies in order to suit their own needs.

Hoovering - Named after the Hoover Vacuum, it is a tactic used to "suck back in" the victim by exhibiting improved or desirable behavior.

Normalizing – A tactic used to desensitize a person to inappropriate or abusive behaviors; manipulating a person to agree or accept something that is in conflict with the law, social norms, or their own basic code of behavior.

Supply – A narcissist's insatiable need to gain the attention and adoration of others for the purpose of building them up and confirming their false sense of superiority and entitlement. (Like my story) He was charismatic and charming to others.

This is someone else's story, but it mirrors my own experience:

I soon became exhausted, focusing solely on getting through each day. I blamed everything on myself. He said **it was** because of me. He compared me with other mothers, saying I should be able to handle everything. Kids, job, home (in my case so he could go do things with HIS friends) while I took care of absolutely everything else.

Someone else's story:

Ambient Abuse – The stealthy, subtle, underground currents of maltreatment that sometimes go unnoticed even by the victims themselves until it is too late; the fostering and enhancement of an atmosphere of intimidation, fear, and instability; often viewed as the most dangerous type of abuse.

He never hit me. On several occasions he placed his hands around my neck, professing his love while squeezing, whispering how he could kill me he loved me so much. He always let go just as I got dizzy and then would break down and cry promising to never hurt me.

Then he would say how lucky I was to have a man who loved me so much and who put up with me. And then there was what they call:

Gas lighting – a form of mental abuse that includes brainwashing or convincing a mentally healthy individual that their understanding of reality is false. In this scenario the abuser is trying to make the victim doubt their own memory, perception, and sanity. In my scenario this also applies: I became more isolated and he would hover when I got a phone call. He wanted to control every aspect of who I talked to and who I would see without him.

Projection – A psychological defense mechanism where a person "projects" their own undesirable thoughts, feelings, or actions onto someone else in order to seek acquittal from their own conscience; example: accusing the victim of cheating when the accuser is actually the one cheating.   And the story goes on: Days, months, years passed and more and more he began walking around me. Ignoring me, even at the dinner table when he ate the food I had prepared and I sat at the other end. His presence was felt only in the small breeze that walking by me caused, as if I weren't a human being but instead a piece of furniture.

Silent Treatment – A preferred weapon of Narcissists; a passive-aggressive form of emotional abuse in which displeasure, disapproval, and contempt exhibited through nonverbal gestures, such as glaring, while maintaining verbal silence.

Someone else's story: She said: "The last two years I put myself to sleep to avoid all feeling. That way, even when I knew he was lying or when I found out about something he had done, it made it easier. Forces were at work to keep me numb and silent and weakened. "

I can relate to the numbing as you have read about in my experience.

Other behaviors are the reinforcing such as dosing (small and temporary revivals of the love bombing phase) Denial (denying one's actions even in the face of physical proof) and Bait and switch (luring the victim in with kindness and affection and once they are "hooked" the abuser switches to being demanding, inattentive and cruel)

This story included physical ramifications of being treated in such an abusive way. Examples were: stomachaches, nausea, and panic attacks. In a sort of self- induced coma, daily life took on a dream quality which softened the edges. But then she went to see a psychologist who was an expert on the Narcissistic Personality Disordered person.

Narcissistic Personality Disorder is a disorder in which the individual has a distorted self-image, unstable and intense emotions, is overly preoccupied with vanity, prestige, power and personal adequacy who also lacks empathy, and has an exaggerated sense of superiority. Narcissistic Personality Disorder is closely associated with egocentrism – a personality characteristic in which people see themselves and their interests and opinions as the only ones that really matter.

I know from my own experience that counseling helped me understand. Educating myself about the different reality my spouse lived in and that it was not my own reality helped me see it was not my fault and it truly was his.

I was able to forgive myself for the waste of time that I had always regretted and I am still working on forgiving myself when it comes to subjecting my child to such an example of a man and of a marriage. We have come far since we removed ourselves from the past.

Chapter Seven
Costs of verbal abuse

The physical manifestations of living in this kind of situation can be many. By the time I was in my early thirty's I had headaches, I needed Tums frequently and my whole body hurt from tension. I thought my god, if I feel like this now (I was in pain every day) how am I going to feel when I am older? I had no idea at this point why I felt the way I did physically. I worked hard in front of a computer every day, I ran a business. I thought my physical troubles had come from long days working, keeping a home and raising my son. I started seeing a massage therapist who gradually made me feel more like a human again. She is the best! She not only worked out all of the knots in my body, she was patient and kind enough to listen to my nightmare along with the counselors I worked with over the years.

When I began to express to others some of the things that went on in my home life I began to see that I was not nuts. This type of treatment was not normal and I did not deserve to be treated this way. I had been putting up with it for seven years at this point. I had asked myself the question "Why do I feel so bad; he doesn't hit me? five years into it. By the seventh year I had been in counseling for two years. I ended up working with this wonderful counselor for a total of three years. She was to help me grow up and to begin to ask for change at home.

I began to feel more connected to myself, to notice the dynamics of my relationship. I began to "not play" the game with Sam. I could walk away sometimes when he would verbally attack me. Or, I could limit the engagement by saying "I don't deserve to be talked to like that please stop it." It was a slow and agonizing process. I began to feel stronger emotionally and physically. There was something good about finding out what was wrong. It made a difference to know that words were really hurting me and stopping them would help me. Such a simple concept. Becoming aware and becoming UN NUMB was like waking up from a very long sleep as I began to notice what and who I was really living with.

Ultimately after I divorced this man and began a new life I would compare coming out of it like I had been swimming under water and had now come up for air. When I looked around at last, especially outside my world had returned to three dimensional colors, it had texture and feeling and it was wonderful. But, it took some time and work to get there.

This is such a simple concept but if you have never been able to stand up for yourself, never been strong enough to realize what was happening to you and find the knowledge that you have the ability to not engage with these behaviors and ask for something else like respect this is actually a huge concept to gain insight into.

The cost, the largest saddest part of this type of life for the abused person is the change in loss of self-esteem. The repercussions and effects of being treated with so little regard and respect can be self-doubt, loss of self-confidence, feeling stuck, on the fence about making decisions of any kind, losing the feelings of joy and happiness because you are always on guard, feeling like everything is your fault or that something is wrong with you, incorporating every negative message given to you into yourself and letting his definition of you define you.

You begin to go over and over incidents in your mind trying to find where you went wrong and what you can do better to make the outcome better the next time. This was the living in my head scenario to the point that I missed living in the moment, missed so much because I was becoming numb. This was the only way to get through it, trying to ignore and overlook while I tried to work, take care of a home and child. There was so much anxiety and fear involved in this situation.

I was in an addictive relationship because this became "normal" to me over time. He tried to control while I tried to fix it. The trouble is that it only gets worse, never better without change. This life seemed like I was a hamster caught in a cage forever spinning the wheel. My view of the world at one time had been that people are basically good and I treated people the way I wanted to be treated. I believed that if you treated people with respect, if you were nice and kind you would receive the same in return. Yes, this was naïve but I liked seeing the world through my rose colored glasses... This made living in it more pleasant for me and I hope the people I encountered.

After this relationship I was never sure that I could trust anyone. I did not believe that what you see is what you get. I certainly needed an update on my views of the world. I am now more careful about who I let in and who I will get close to. That is good for me to a certain extent because I no longer have a sign on my forehead that says, take advantage of my kindness, walk on me as much as you like. I still greet the world in a friendly way but I am a little wary. I think I needed to learn to be a little less open anyway. I have learned to have boundaries and I have learned to only do what I want to for or with someone. I no longer let people take advantage of me. I have learned to say no. Better late than never.

In the beginning of this relationship Sam and I were friends. Over time after knowing this man for seven years we both were divorced at this point, we began to date. I lived with this man for a period of time and then we mutually decided it would not work. I went back to my home town. While there I went for a visits with family. While there I had a change of heart. Sam and I got together to talk. We talked about what in our relationship needed work. We tried to come up with solutions and a plan to work it out. I decided to give the relationship another try even though in my gut I thought this was not really the man for me.

I truly was a young woman at this point and was easily influenced by what family and friends said and what they thought. So, I went back for more. The thing is Sam went back and forth even then about his commitment to me. He had not wanted to raise more children and I had a son who he also went back and forth about. He would act like a good father one minute and then he would be mean, even cruel towards me and my son. What happened eventually and the price I was to pay revolved around my son. The conflict in our home was never lost on my son. He was to spend most of his childhood watching the dynamics of a relationship that was toxic. He was to be the one witness to our very bad times. Don't forget, there were good times mixed in there as in any marriage but it took a supreme effort to maintain those days. Relationships and life are not supposed to be that difficult.

In my own mind I made assumptions that somehow my son could decipher what was "normal" and good and what was not. I could not have been more wrong. My son was learning that this must be the way to treat women in the privacy of the home and that somehow every bad time he witnessed must have been my fault. He lived with the constant tension and tried to stay under the radar. He knew this dynamic was wrong and would periodically say to me "mom why is he so mean, why don't you leave him?" If Sam was making me crazy and I was supposed to know better how do you think this affected my son?

I did leave briefly when my son was almost eleven because I had had enough or so I thought. I was hoping my leaving would wake Sam up to what he could lose. It turned out that I was not strong enough yet to stay gone. My livelihood was intertwined with this man; my life was so intermingled by then I was not yet prepared to handle everything on my own. I also did not know how to ask for and find help.

By the time my son was fourteen he began to act out some of his anger. He wanted to leave and run away from this situation. Who could blame him? The cost to my child was enormous. As much as I tried to balance this out for him by trying to model a strong person and strong work ethic and trying to treat people in a kind way and so on, he also saw exactly the opposite behaviors. This teeter totter was so out of balance I am surprised that anyone in our home was able to hang on.

What Have I lost?

What have I lost in my life along the way, along the path of verbal abuse?

As a human being I have lost dignity, self-esteem, and direction. I have been afraid to make the wrong decisions, every one being difficult to choose, fear of choosing the wrong one. Stuck on a fence, always because I was afraid. What is so wrong with me that I deserve to be treated this way I wondered? I have felt depressed, lonely, deeply in pain not knowing why until the question comes to mind at last... why do I feel so bad? He doesn't hit me. I am wrong – he hits me with a barrage of words that are meant to kill my spirit, my mind, my independence, my feeling of strength and freedom. My courage to make good decisions, filling me with doubt and despair.

I have felt that somehow I have been the one at fault. If only I could have done better. If only I could know the right things to say, to do. If I could get it right, then he wouldn't treat me so poorly. Or would he anyway? Long ago things put away years ago. I repeat parts of my journey so it can be recognized for what it was.

Then comes the dawn. No matter what I would have done I would have been treated like I don't matter. The things I lost, the most important thing I lost because I left too late was the respect of my son for a time. He saw and learned from the verbal abuse.

What he learned was he had to choose not to repeat the same things and to not pass this behavior down in his own life.   Even though I divorced the man who treated me so poorly, it was too late. Or was it?

What I had as my son grew through adolescence was a son who thought everything was my fault. Or so it seemed. My son saw how his father treated me, he saw and felt how my husband treated him. Somehow in all of this my son had mixed messages which confused how he felt. What he saw as a role model, how a man treats his wife was also mixed messages. My son I think blamed me for not taking this treatment passively so that it would stop (or so he thought). In my son's adolescent anger for a while he thought it was ok to treat me poorly, that I deserved to be yelled at, put down and criticized and disrespected. I held my ground. This is often how teenage boys act out. And then with time he figured it out. He was torn because he knew we were in this together, he knew it was not right. My son asked me when he was about 12, he said "mom why is he so mean?" And, "why do you stay with him?" This was not the first time he had said this to me.

What it seemed I had lost was the thing I was trying to gain, that is self-esteem for my son, dignity, without loneliness and despair.   Now I have self-esteem, I am strong and independent. I know I have worth and courage. I fought so hard to show my son the opposite side of this equation, that he should be kind to people, that I always had his back, that it is never ok to be mean to others. He knows in his heart of hearts, but I left too late. In leaving late it makes it harder for your children to work all of this through and to come out on the other side. But, he did.

It would take a long time in the process of my son's growth and self-discovery to put away his anger, to feel pride in what he accomplishes, to feel the happiness and joy he can bring to himself. For a very long time my son decided it was easier to bury his feelings so it would not hurt so badly when he was the object of verbal abuse.   There were times as we both recovered from the onslaught that I wished my son could know, and maybe remember that I tried to shield him from harm. Instead he must have just wanted me to shut up and take the words without argument so they would stop. But, what he did not know then, but does now is that the words would have come anyway, they were not my fault, and they were not his fault. All I was looking for was love and respect because that is what I had to give. I could divorce my husband and did. I could not and did not walk away from my son. Instead I held onto the rope that I had thrown him years before waiting for him to cross over, knowing that we would not stay in this forever.

I had tried to shield his body and soul from the onslaught, taking as much of the pain in so that the words would leave him alone. He was a child. How could he know that this was not normal? I did not know that what I could lose, instead of my own self, my own soul which belong to me now, that I could have and almost lost the person I loved more than myself, my son. Don't do this... please... ask for change and if change is impossible leave before it is too late.

Chapter 8

Why I stayed

Lest you think I was a completely nuts for staying you have to keep in mind that the flip side of this story is the man I was with had a nice side. The nice guy returned periodically to keep me guessing, to keep me off balance and to keep me from leaving.

As I mentioned, Sam could be the most charming man in public, but there were just enough times where in private this man gave me attention, expressions of care and concern or love so I thought I was getting somewhere in initiating that "real" connection I thought I lost and just could not find.

I hoped every day that things would go well. I hoped every day to find the key to unlock and forever keep the nice part of this man with me. Brief glimpses were what I lived on. Just enough (those scraps I mentioned a few chapters ago) to keep me hanging in there, just enough to ensure I would stay in it. Just enough attention to carry this game on. I know for a fact that he would have continued this game FOREVER. I think that if I had wanted to continue in this relationship he could have still been my husband today. This relationship was working for him. It was me who had to say Uncle, it was me who had to tell him where the door was. It took time for me to gather my strength because I had become pathetic in my own eyes.

In my experience, my partner and I had lunch together frequently. These lunches were like the way we were when we first became friends. These conversations were about business so were safe ground on which to meet. This was our common ground. It was when we got home in our private time that we had so much trouble.

We did go places together and we had days we enjoyed each other's company. We took trips to arts and crafts shows, went out to dinner, went to movies and did all of the normal things that couples do. Sometimes we had days without incident.

My partner would give me lovely cards for Valentine's Day, Anniversary, and Birthday and so on. He always professed to love me more than anyone else ever could or would. I believed him. I had never loved anyone more either. I loved the nice version of this man with all of my heart, and as much as I was capable of up to this point. This man would praise me on occasion when it came to business. He would compliment my intelligence and if we had gone out together he would talk about how pretty or nice he thought I was. He had nick names for me that were affectionate and personal. Sometimes he would hold my hand if ever so lightly. It always seemed that if he actually held on to my hand tightly that it would somehow let me know that he really did like me. So, it was always a tentative hold. Sometimes I would squeeze his hand wanting for him to hold my hand more tightly. This was a mistake because more often than not, this would cause him to completely drop my hand and walk slightly ahead of me. His message was very clear at these moments, "Don't ask for more and I am in charge."

I was always (mostly) optimistic about getting to the day where this misunderstanding between us would be realized and talked out. At last all of our issues would be resolved if only I could get him to understand how I looked at life and our relationship and that what I wanted was a real connection and love. I wanted to create a loving family unit where we could use our words. I am certain Sam knew this about me and so he went about making sure this was something I would never have. Remember too that my partner did go to counseling periodically with me for me, us and our child. He could talk circles around most of the counselors we saw. Sam was just smart enough to tell a story about our relationship that painted me as the problem. At one point I had one counselor say to me, "Do you realize he thinks he is the victim in this scenario?" I was floored. I had seen myself as the victim in our relationship by this time. What? I could not believe it.

My partner said the words I love you almost every day. He would have talks with me when I asked for them to try to discuss what might help us in our relationship. I can recall sitting in the living room and telling him what I thought, how I felt and what we could do to improve our relationship. He would calmly listen, tell me he would do his part and work on how he spoke to me, he would try to connect with me, be intimate with me. We would get up hug, and walk away, go about our day. He always promised to do better.

He had me fooled and confused. In business I was his partner; at home I was his for show when needed to take me to events with friends. I was his to own, control and laugh at if I fell for his put downs. He was amused if he could see that he had hurt me or confused me.

If I fell into the trap, believing I could share my hopes or dreams for myself with him this would be his cue to discourage me, to invalidate my desires, making what I wanted seem petty and inconsequential. This was his cue to undermine and try to make me feel weak. How could I possibly accomplish all of the things I would share with him about what I wanted to make myself happy independently from him? It was his most expert opinion that I had all I could handle and I was crazy to try to do anything else. Inside the box I was. I stayed because I felt that change could so easily be achieved. I stayed because something better was just around the corner of our relationship. I stayed because my business was intertwined with this man and I had a son who needed a father. I had so much time and energy invested and I did not want to be divorced.   I was stuck on the proverbial fence of knowing there was more and that I needed more, deserved more, but I was telling myself to be grateful for what I had.   I was telling myself to lower my expectations and to try to live with it (keep sucking it up). It was exhausting.

One of the major issues we had between us and the elephant in the room had to do with whether or not I could or would have more children. Early on in our relationship Sam led me to believe that this might be a possibility. He seemed to know how important it was to me. We renegotiated this along the way several times. I tried to be grateful for what I had. One son whom I loved with all my heart. Somewhere along the way (after I had been in counseling for a year) I began to see and then ask for what I needed. I also began to see how limiting this marriage was.

Somewhere in my subconscious I began to think that having another child would be the only way I could possibly have enough love in my life. As I said I had always wanted at least two children about six years apart so that I could give each one the attention they deserved.   I would have another person to love who would allow me to love them. This could and would be how I could make it through this situation. Faulty thinking to be sure, but many other women have babies to try and save relationships, make them better and then there are those who try and make a man stay by having a child. All faulty thinking, but that goes to show how many women have been out there just trying to find someone who might love them. Self-esteem to be given from others. If we are lovable to someone else, we can be ok we think. Not. I love myself and I deserve someone who will value me at least as much as I do myself.

I also thought that having a baby could bring Sam and I together. Once again, if only we could ever be on the same page. He was 13 years older than I. He was old school thinking and believed he was too old to be a father. We had a seven-year-old at home. He already was a father. I told Sam that if he truly loved me enough he would understand and ultimately would be happier than he had ever been with a child because he would be around. He had missed his first two daughters' childhoods because he was always working. I again brought up the subject of wanting more children. I told Sam that I had tried to not want more, but had not succeeded. I had always wanted two children. It was in my bones; it was part of who I am. I wanted another child and I was certain that Sam would love this child too. The timing of this was four years into our marriage and roughly one year after I began counseling. When Sam realized I was serious about this he began to reassert his control. Now our chess game began in earnest.

What follows is a very personal part of my story. I felt it important to include so that you can see or I can demonstrate through this story the extent to which I struggled with this man and this relationship. Perhaps it will help you to not feel alone. People do things that may seem crazy to others inside marriages. Not only were Sam and I having a wrist wrestling match about who was in charge (I wanted an equal partnership not power over) we also were to have a struggle about my body and who was in charge of that.

As I said, when I met this man and began a friendship with him and then a closer relationship with him in order to get me to take the bait (move in, marry him, have a long term relationship with him) Sam had to make me believe there was a chance, or I would have an opportunity to have a second child with him. I married Sam believing that if it came up that we could figure it out together. After our son was about to turn 7 I began to tell Sam that I could not put the desire for another child aside. I had tried and because I had a less than desirable connection to Sam who would not want to add more love to their life by having a wonderful child?

At first in discussions Sam was tentative and acted like he cared about my needs. After the discussion it was not mentioned again by him because I think he felt if he could ignore it and out last me until I hit menopause he would have won the issue. His stance was no more children. The only trouble was that menopause was many years away. I was only 33 at the time.

I talked with my grandmother and told her we might want another child. She said "Well you had better hurry up." In 1990 my grandmother passed away. I had never lost anyone before and I was devastated at her loss. I tried to consider why we are here at all. My answer was our connections to each other and love are where the meaning to life is. I knew I wanted better connections and relationships with my family and within my marriage. I still wanted another child. I could literally feel this person waiting to come into actual being. This is how strongly I felt about having another child. I had tried to suppress the desire and to ignore what I had always known was a part of my being and a part of my soul. I became pregnant in 1991 and then suffered a miscarriage in my second month. The stress did not help.

The day I lost this pregnancy I had gotten up and just did not feel right. My body felt tired and sluggish. Sam and I were getting ready to go out to lunch. Instead we went to my Doctor's office where they performed an ultrasound. As they tried to tell me what was about to happen I was alone. Sam had dropped me off here to go pick up our son. He took our son to the dentist and dropped him off there (the dentists were good friends). That way he could come back and pick me up. When he returned to pick me up I told him I apparently was having a miscarriage. I got in the car and put my feet up on the dash. Anyone who knows what it is like to lose a baby this way knows you try to do anything you can to stop it or to keep this from happening.

Even if there was no hope I could not give up. So I put my feet up on the dash. We stopped to pick up our son at the dentist as it was on the way home. Sam left me in the car while he went to get our son. Me with my feet up on the dash in December. He stayed gone for a really long time knowing I was in distress with my feet up on the dash as he took his time to get our son. He was inside talking while I sat in the car. When we finally got home I laid in bed hoping this would not happen. It did. I was again alone.

After this Sam tried to tell me everything would be ok and I could try again. When the Doctor cleared me to try again Sam said "No, don't you ever do this again."

I put my feelings aside for the next couple of years to take a step back and rethink everything. After the miscarriage I left for a short time. I was not ready to leave yet. The struggle about having more children was to last until January 1995 when I became pregnant with my second son.

As many women have done before me I got pregnant without permission (yes I said permission) from my husband. How did I get here and how was this passed down as normal?

Domestic Violence is frequently passed down in one form or another from generation to generation. In some families if there is even one person who is not in control of their emotions or self-aware enough to see what anger and physical violence is doing to their other family members and if it continues throughout a child's upbringing the child has a few choices about how he or she will be as they go through their own lives.

I know that in my mother's family her father had a difficult time with anger. He was not taught to use words when his frustration level became too much. I think that this can translate to children who are always watching, how to act as an adult. Unless children are consciously aware as adults and are introspective, maybe they get counseling and learn how to resolve conflict the choices they have are to repeat the behaviors in their own families or get help to make the appropriate changes so they can learn to deal with their own emotions in the moment (which is what one needs when dealing with children) or they can check out all - together using alcohol or other substances to become numb themselves.

When an ever powerful adult reacts with rage over spilled milk at the dinner table and overreacts to any small thing that a child can do as they learn, it is very scary for the child. Talking to a child through gritted teeth because the rage is visible and spills out in this way creates fear. Family violence is passed down frequently. When a parent does not know how to cope with their own feelings of frustration and loss of control it can be a frequent thing to strike out against those nearest to them.

If children live with an anger addict this is what they learn to model so that they feel in control. Children as witnesses also learn that maybe this is "normal" and maybe life is like this at other homes. It is never talked about and we never breathe a word to anyone. We all pretend all is just fine at home. Unless the cops are called.

Over time and back in the day people were not taught Anger Management or how to deal with emotions especially explosive emotions. Add to this that corporal punishment was common and children were spanked, seen and not heard or sometimes even beaten in the privacy of their homes without consequence you have generations who felt that manipulation and power over a family including the other adult in the home (the wife) was common.

People did not talk about what might be wrong or what caused this hyper reaction to frustration or worry. Many times fathers or even mothers grew up in an environment where beating your children was "normal." It is supposedly no longer allowed as our society has evolved people are even afraid to spank their child for fear someone will accuse them of child endangerment or neglect. People lose their children over much less violent offenses. But, back a generation or two these things were not discussed and it was allowed.

As a child when an adult hurts you it causes so many feelings of confusion. It is so damaging to the soul to have a parent strike you physically. As the child grows into a man or (woman) and no one teaches him anything different he will many times become the perpetrator of the family violence even though he knows this is not good.

The repercussions of living in this environment are so many. The feeling of impending doom or waiting at any moment for something horrible to happen. Feelings of powerlessness and feeling unloved or inconsequential are common. Post-Traumatic Stress and anxiety or panic attack as well as fear are among the possibilities of the collateral damages that children are left with who have come from homes with anger and violence.

My reasons for mentioning these issues are because when a female child in particular is raised in this environment often she chooses a mate and a relationship that will recreate the home she grew up in. This is not intentional of course. There was no healthy role model to show her a different kind of relationship.

The fear that a child carries when they cannot depend on a parent to protect them, calm them, talk to them or even be stable enough to be able to predict any consistent behavior is enormous.

Hopefully what I have communicated here is that the family violence passed down from generation to generation reverberates and ripples touching everyone in the family and beyond.

So back to my situation……

Slowly I began to see, hear and feel the reality of my verbally abusive situation. This is why I called it uncomfortably numb. I had learned to become numb to not only how I was treated slowly and consistently from the beginning of this relationship, (specifically after I married him); I had also learned to not feel my feelings and sort of disassociate from them to survive in this toxic atmosphere.

I began to work through all of this as a young adult when I began to see a counselor. Counseling saved my life really. I grew up and began to mature in my early thirties after many hours spent in therapy. I recommend it.

When a child is raised in a toxic environment no one walks away from the experience unscathed. We all have choices. At least conscious choices are there to be examined and then carefully picked or not picked. Paths to go down or not go down. There are so many things we do unconsciously so many mistakes and bad choices that we can't know or realize because we are repeating a pattern and choosing what is known to us or what feels normal.

So many people from this time period had no idea, no inkling that hitting a child, hurting a child by actions physically or words spoken was wounding their children for life. There are those who continue these behaviors even in the 21st century because even though they may have heard how damaging it is they do not know another way. They are simply repeating the patterns they know and believe to be "normal."

Physical abuse: Why She Stays

Many women don't stay especially when they are physically battered. Women leave and shelters are usually full. Leaving is a process. Many times for a battered woman the violence escalates when a woman does leave.

In almost all of domestic violence homicides the woman had left the perpetrator, was about to leave or had given him good cause to believe she would be leaving. Some battered women are a prisoner in their own homes.

Emotional abuse occurs in virtually all relationships where physical violence exists. A constant barrage of verbal abuse wears down the woman's resistance, making it more difficult for her to leave.

Some battered women stay because they believe that counseling will help their batterers stop the violent behaviors. "Anger management classes are often totally useless for the men who commit not only emotional/verbal abuse but who physically strike out against their mates. The classes are based on the thoroughly discredited idea that batterers lost their temper and strike out. Assailant's violent behavior is typically planned (instrumental) not impulsive. The anger assumption leads to a lot of terrible public and program policy that is designed to placate and avoid making the batterer angry rather than holding him accountable."

Most experts agree that a man must be violence free for two to three years before counseling is safe or appropriate.

Some women stay because they hold out hope for change. Change not only in ceasing physical violence, but they may even believe it is possible for the verbal and emotional terrorism to stop. I have to repeat again that when a spouse or partner is abusive in these ways there is little hope for real change because the partner who uses violence and emotional abuse against a partner lives in a different reality. He does not want to change most of the time. This is what he knows and this is what has worked for him.

Some women stay because they perceive they cannot afford justice (a lawyer) to help them with civil protection orders or sometimes a perpetrator may be able to afford a better attorney and threatens he will take away the children involved. Battered women stay for their children.

Some stay because there is no place to go. Some places do not have shelters. If they do exist often the funding is in constant danger.

There are so many reasons why a woman stays or why it takes preparation and a change within her to be able to remove herself and her children if she has them from this situation.

Many women lack support from others.

NO MORE

"In one year alone 12.7 million men and women in the U.S. are physically abused, raped or stalked by their partners. That is approximately the number of people in New York City and Los Angeles combined. That is 24 people every minute. These are people we know. It is time to end the silence and shame for good. Like the peace sign, the yellow "support our troops" ribbon or the red AIDSA ribbon, the goal of NO MORE is to raise visibility for these issues, challenging the stigma that surrounds them, and taking the first step toward broader social change. NCADV supports the NO

MORE project and we encourage you to check them out online at www.nomore.org"

For the younger generations to contemplate Cycle of Domestic Violence Continues in Generation Y
Dallas Business Wire

"Young women who were in shelters as children are now seeking protection from domestic violence situations themselves according to the 2013 Mary Kay Truth About Abuse Survey. The annual survey takes an in depth look at domestic violence through the perspective of executive directors at women's shelters across the country. Along with the cycle of violence continuing in Generation Y, the 2013 survey reported that many women are staying in shelters for longer periods of time because of limited access to resources. The ripple effect of women staying in shelters for longer periods of time prevents other women from receiving needed assistance. As fewer women are able to seek shelter, more women are staying in or going back to violent and dangerous situations. More than 800 women's shelters across the nation shared their concerns about this pattern with Mary Kay Inc. Key findings include:

"Most shelters are servicing more women, specifically more women between the ages of 18-32 and more women with children. The economy is a factor and is why women stay or go back to their abusers. Mental health issues are prevalent. While many shelters are able to provide emergency housing, most do not have the resources to provide the long term care and rehabilitation that survivors need to ultimately break the cycle."

Chapter 9
So now what?

So now what? I have talked about some of the issues of verbal abuse which is the precursor in my opinion to physical domestic violence. You will have to be the judge in your own situation about whether this relationship can be saved. You will figure that out as you begin to ask for change. You should be able to tell if there is hope for a real relationship with your partner by the reaction of your mate when you do ask for change. Talking to a marriage counselor with your partner if possible or getting into counseling yourself will help you make a determination.

I am afraid that in a lot of cases the asking for change will fall on deaf ears. In fact, the verbal abuse could worsen if your mate feels that he is on the verge of losing control. This is because your mate is very much locked into the pattern that has worked for him for most of his life. Certainly it has worked for some time in the dynamic of your relationship with him. His opinion might be "if it ain't broke don't fix it." If your mate has not wanted to change anything up to this point the odds of any movement on his part are extremely small. That is my opinion. I am sure there will be and can be exceptions to the rule.

In an earlier chapter I mentioned that when the inevitable accusations happened where my mate would verbally attack me, I began to stop defending myself. I would not verbally spar with this man any more. It took practice but I began to say "please stop talking to me like that, I don't deserve it." If he continued the verbal attack, I would walk out of the room. You certainly can try to speak with this person when things are calm and you can try to set up new ground rules for behavior. Again, I am certain this must help some people especially when these constructive conversations are in addition to trips to a counselor of some kind. I did try counseling with and without my mate.

Ultimately all of the talking in the world did not or could not help our dynamic. In this man's heart of hearts, he did love me the only way he knew how. His type of love and my type of love did not meet anywhere close to what I needed to continue to live. What I learned about relationships that came hard was this. My partner lived in his own reality. He really thought this was how to have a long term relationship.

This dynamic must have worked in his childhood home so he repeated the behaviors his father must have modeled about marriage. His father was most definitely in charge and back in the day there was no question about it. His mother suffered from low self-esteem. She did not work outside the home. I do know that she would not allow anyone to take her picture because she felt she was so unattractive. When Sam's father died in his late 60's within 6 months his mother died too. She was so connected to this relationship and with no children left to raise, no career and no husband she was lost. She just died on the street one day while window shopping.

In the life span of fifteen years of my relationship with this man, we saw countless counselors regarding various issues and were always on a different page or opposing sides. We had one counselor tell us "I don't know how to help you." The majority of counselors we saw were ironically, men. The last counselor I was to see mostly on my own was a woman. The first trip in I told her my objective which was to ask for her help in getting out of this relationship. As we talked we decided to give Sam an opportunity to come in too to see if there might be any way to work this out or save this relationship. The counselor could tell that my heart was broken, that I loved some version of this man with all my heart but that it had become a matter of my survival. I deserved to be treated with respect and care by my partner in my own home. Could this ever be accomplished with this man or was it hopeless? We set out to find the answer.

My counselor saw the charming good guy I had initially met. She looked carefully and listened carefully as she watched us interact as a couple. At first everything seemed as the rest of the world saw us. A couple with troubles, but who ultimately did love each other. As we started to delve further into the dynamics of the interactions, as we discussed our conflicts over how to raise children, how much work I did around the house and at work, things that could be done to make each of us happier and more content, the counselor began to see that when I was uncomfortable or when I was sad, or had an emotional reaction to what was said, the mask my partner held on his face began to slip.

Under it she saw the unmistakable expression of amusement, and even enjoyment in watching me squirm. She saw what I had been talking about; this was how he got his kicks. He enjoyed putting me down and complaining about me to someone else and also enjoyed it when I felt bad. He was caught! Our counselor said you are right he is exactly what you have said. Sam was a narcissistic person who had no empathy for others. He enjoyed the game.

For me it became a chess game. At the end I decided what I could give up and what I could not.

When things got too heavy, when our counselor tried to call him on any of his negative behaviors my partner stopped coming to the counselor anymore. If he was capable of change at all it did not matter because he would not even attempt to try. He was to have none of it. He would criticize me for going to see a counselor. He thought it was weak. I think he was probably afraid if I continued to go he would lose his power and control over me. He was correct in thinking this. It was never stated out loud. I continued to go and talk about strategies.

I need to say here that the fact that we lived in completely different realities made it totally impossible for me to get what I needed from this relationship. I am sure he was not getting what he wanted either. He wanted power and control over me and it was slipping through his fingers. The stronger I got the more boundaries I learned to put around myself and my self-esteem drew us further apart. We lived on different planets by the end of our marriage. He did not have a clue how to do a real equal partnership with a loving woman. As I became stronger and began loving myself I would not and could not let anyone treat me as though I was inconsequential. I could no longer allow anyone to treat me with sarcasm, dismissiveness, disdain, sneering looks or remarks. The list is very long when it came to what I could no longer live with. All of the ways I had tried to defend myself to this man who had said he loved me stopped. I no longer had to defend my life, my existence. The game no longer worked for me. I got off the teeter totter and as you know one cannot teeter totter alone.

Sam could never have given me what I needed and wanted from a relationship because he did not know how to give "IT," and did not want to anyway. Once I got this point finally after fifteen years of struggle Sam knew and I knew that our marriage was over. The addiction to the relationship was a little harder to acknowledge and to let die. It can be done! Life is way too short to live with a person who does not value you and think that you are wonderful.

Eventually, the thing that was the final straw for me was not the verbal abuse; it was how he acted out his loss of control in our relationship. He began to sabotage our business by talking money out of it to gamble. In typical fashion I tried to ignore how much money he was wasting for quite a long time. At the end he was taking enough out to make it difficult to pay the mortgage. I finally said; please go find somewhere else to stay. I said please go now, do not wait, go stay with a friend. You have to stop wasting our money. I thought he would finally get it because we were at last separated. For the next three years we would be separated. I would wait for any sign of change from him. I don't know what he was waiting for. He would see our children. There were a few times we went out to dinner or to take our little boy to the movies. When we went out on "dates" together they were reminiscent of the time I mentioned where he would keep his distance. He kept asking to come home. I would say "what has changed?"

Once Sam did come home once for two months. One of our children had been hurt and hospitalized so he came home and was supportive. He came in the fall and stayed until right after Christmas. He slept down the hall in another room keeping his distance and his control. Then one day he left for work and never came back. He went back to his apartment. We did not talk about it at the time.

There was one more time he came by and for the first time in years kissed me with some of the passion I had felt years and years before. It was to be the last time. After that he said again he wanted to come home. I finally said alright in a tentative fashion. My mother was coming for a visit that weekend so I said we should wait to move his things until she had gone. After the weekend was over he never moved back in. We did not discuss it. He knew and I knew that nothing had changed. I think we both knew our power struggle could have continued on making neither of us happy. It was finally over for all intents and purposes.

We had separated after 15 years in the same house. The leaving and letting go experience for both of us took the next three years. Sam used one last power play on me. He refused to sign the divorce papers until I put our house up for sale. I think his attitude was that if he could not live there he was not going to let me stay there either. I put the house up for sale and in the back of my mind I thought after he signs the papers I can change my mind about selling it. Sam won that argument ultimately. I think it was good to let go of all of the memories that were in that house. Losing the house hurt and I miss it to this day but I have a different wonderful place to be with a new husband that I love dearly.

Sam and I still had conversations on the phone about kids and he would still try to rip me to shreds in a sentence or at worst a paragraph. It continued to work on occasion with my hanging up feeling defeated and hurt. It took until 2006 for me to hang up the phone with him, searching my gut, my heart and my soul to see if I was still intact. I hung up thinking, how am I? Did I get what I wanted from the conversation? Did he cause me pain or hurt in any way? Did he make me feel bad? The answer was no he had not hurt me I had not allowed it. Yes, I had gotten what I wanted from the conversation. I did not feel bad and he had had no effect on how I felt about myself at that moment. I could not believe it. I had accomplished enough growth and developed enough self-esteem and enough boundaries that at last I was free from this man.

Not long after that, we did not hear from him anymore. He dropped off the planet and decided not to have contact with me or the two sons that we had been raising. It used to make me angry because I worried about their reaction to being left behind by this man. How does a dad do this? I could live without him but I worried about the repercussions or possible abandonment issues they could end up with. This was most probably his final way of disturbing me (us). By disappearing he definitely had the last word.

Chapter 10
The conspiracy of silence

The expression conspiracy of silence, or culture of silence, relates to a condition or matter which is known to exist, but by tacit communal unspoken consensus is not talked about or acknowledged. Commonly such matters are considered culturally shameful. (Wikipedia.org) In addition the definition states:

Avoidance of recognition of some problem in order to officially bury (hide) a possible problem and thus avoid accusations, investigations or liability. (Wikipedia.org)

Often women do not speak to each other about verbal abuse because this subject creates shame for the woman. The silence is universal shared by both men and women. Women keep silent as though verbal abuse is her fault. I immediately think of comparisons to rape and blaming the victim. Our society used to put a woman's past on trial when trying a man for rape. Society was trying to assign who could be to blame for this violent crime against a woman. Recently a woman was blamed for her own rape because she had worn "skinny" jeans. It was said the sex had to be consensual because she had to help the perpetrator get her jeans off. Ever heard the expression by force or fear? I am certain this woman was in an extreme state of fear. Yet, the system blamed her for wearing skinny jeans.   We now stand together on Denim Day each year. I am proud to say I was given a denim rose to wear to make a statement against sexual assault a couple of years ago. Here is the story:

In Italy, an 18-year-old girl was raped by her driving instructor. He was found guilty. The guilty verdict was overturned. When the decision was overturned, the Chief Judge argued, "because the victim wore very, very tight jeans, she had to have helped him remove them, and by removing the jeans it was no longer rape but consensual sex." Denim Day is a day to bring awareness to sexual assault by displaying denim in ANY fashion, whether wearing jeans or a denim rose pin. Wear denim on Denim Day each year to help spread the word. If you or someone you know has been sexually assaulted, please contact SARA (Sexual Assault Response Advocates) Advocates in Nevada 775-883-7654 or to ask for help please contact some of the resources provided in this book. There is help available in every state. Contact women's centers or google help in your area.

The same types of stigma are attached to the most intimate relationships between men and women. There are men who feel it is "normal" to use verbal put downs to control their wives. There are many wives who are ashamed and who do not want to discuss, admit or share that this is happening to them. We only hear about it after they have been physically hurt by their partners.

It is my opinion that there is a deafening conspiracy of silence in our country and most certainly in other countries when it comes to the subject of verbal abuse. Why is this so? This is the "normal" in our societies. What are we teaching our daughters? What are we teaching our sons?

Effects of a conspiracy of silence:

Those who have suffered have their suffering extended by having their condition ignored or minimized, and are not considered seriously or redressed appropriately.

Lessons that might be learned for future are not learned.

Those who are directly suffering, or causing others to suffer, perpetuate their cycle of harm and suffering passing this legacy down from generation to generation.

In the Western world both the proverb and the image are often used to refer to a lack of moral responsibility on the part of people who refuse to acknowledge impropriety, looking the other way or feigning ignorance.

Part of the conditioning of women has components teaching her to minimize her negative experiences with men in day to day interactions. If every woman complained about every injustice every day, the sound would be deafening. No one would take us seriously on a one to one case by case basis. It becomes sort of like crying wolf. So, we save up for the times that really matter, sucking it up in between. I generalize as though most women have experienced injustice and discrimination by the world. For those women who have never had this experience please forgive my generalizing. For those of you who can identify with what I am talking about I thank you for listening to my rant. There are those who would control every aspect of women including trying to control our bodies. In some (most) parts of the world men try to control women's bodies as well as their minds.

By not having access to educating one's mind is the first step in making sure women have no control. In our country there are those who try to control our decisions as women about our own bodies, our own health. There are men and some women who think nothing of interfering in our own choice about whether or when to have a child. The government wants to control our bodies and have made access to health care difficult for many women to find.

Some women become pregnant by accident through failure of birth control or sometimes just poor planning. Some women are not ready to have a child, some should not become mothers. Some women who accidentally become pregnant experience extreme hardships if forced to carry a baby to term and then give it away. Not every woman who accidentally becomes pregnant even in a marriage where they already have plenty of children to raise should be forced to have another child. It is none of the governments business when it comes to making this decision. How did the government become involved in this very personal decision that should only be between the woman, her doctor and her husband if she has one?

Even then, I say that ultimately it is and should be the woman's decision because it is HER body. A woman's body belongs to her and only her. I say this because in my life my husband Sam had tried to control my body. He tried to control my desire for a child; he tried to control whether I had one or when I had one. He tried to control if I breast fed and then complained and tried to get me to stop breastfeeding when he thought I should. He made comments and tried to coerce me to stop.

The marketing of images of women in boxes (literally) as being contained and controlled is done in a subtle way and not so subtly. We don't discuss these images much as a society we just watch. Boxes with women in them remind me of some of the concerns I had in my doomed relationship. There came a time when my partner knew enough about me that he did not want to or need to know more. He knew enough and assumed the rest. It turned out that he had put me in a box metaphorically thinking he knew me not wanting to know more about me. Really knowing me, connecting with me was not essential because I served a purpose and ultimately was a means to his end. My partner needed me to feel like he had power and was in control. He needed me to work in our business and in our home. He needed me in the house even if it was in very separate corners so that he would not feel alone. He could safely put me in a box, knowing I would fit and not make too much noise. I was not essential to his wellbeing really; I was not essential to his existence. I was essential to his appearances in the world as part of a package and part of the illusion he tried to create as a successful, good guy. A good husband, good father and good person in general. That is what he believed then and that is what he most likely believes to this day. He truly did not think he had done anything wrong. This is the paradox. This is why the silence holds.

In a broader sense our society condones the "See No Evil, Hear No Evil, Speak No Evil doctrine when it comes to our treatment of women and not just in other countries, but here in the United States of America. I would call this looking the other way "Willful Blindness."

I do not want to overlook the fact that men are also the victims of verbal abuse and are harassed daily by women who suffer from the same sense of loss of control and the need to feel power and control over her sons, her daughters and her husband or partner. This type of female is teaching her sons and daughters to behave in the same way eventually victimizing others in their partnerships and relationships. But, for all intents and purposes for this book and from my own experience I speak about men who verbally abuse and then sometimes physically abuse women. In either case, there is a better way to live.

In my next relationship I asked that my partner not put me in a box and that he get to know me more and more every day. Keeping the surprises and the learning alive. No more boxes for me.

Incident

I have debated many times about whether to include this article because it is such a tragic story about one woman and her male companion. It is such a violent story and is so solemn a subject that I had considered leaving it out of this book. I find that I cannot because this reality happens around the world. The violence and the utter disregard for human beings is told with absolute clarity here: I warn you though that it is very graphic.

The victims, a 23-year old woman and a male friend, were on their way home on the night of 16 December 2012 after watching the film Life of Pi in Saket in South Delhi. They boarded a chartered bus at Munirka for Dwarka that was being driven by joyriders about 9:30 pm (IST). There were only six others in the bus, including the driver. One of the men, a minor, had called for passengers telling them that the bus was going towards their destination. The woman's friend became suspicious when the bus deviated from its normal route and its doors were shut. When he objected, the group of six men already on board, including the driver, taunted the couple, asking what they were doing alone at such a late hour.

When the woman's friend tried to intervene, he was beaten, gagged and knocked unconscious with an iron rod. The men then dragged the woman to the rear of the bus, beating her with the rod and raping her while the bus driver continued to drive. Medical reports later suggested that the woman suffered serious injuries to her abdomen, intestines and genitals due to the assault, and doctors say that the damage indicates that a blunt object (suspected to be the iron rod) may have been used for penetration. That rod was later described by police as being a rusted, L-shaped implement of the type used as a wheel jack handle.

According to the International Business Times, a police spokesman said that the minor was the most brutal attacker and had "sexually abused his victim twice and ripped out her intestines with his bare hands." According to police reports the woman attempted to fight off her assailants, biting three of the attackers and leaving bite marks on the accused men.

After the beatings and rape ended, the attackers threw both the victims from the moving bus. Then the bus driver allegedly tried to drive the bus over the woman but she was pulled aside by her male friend. One of the perpetrators later cleaned the vehicle to remove evidence. Police impounded it the next day.

The partially clothed victims were found on the road by a passerby at around 11 pm (IST). The passerby phoned the Delhi, who took the couple to <u>Safdarjung Hospital</u> where the female victim was given emergency treatment and placed on mechanical ventilation. She was found with injury marks all over her body and only five percent of her intestines remaining inside of her abdomen. A doctor at the hospital later said that the "rod was inserted into her and it was pulled out with so much force that the act brought out her intestines also. That is probably the only thing that explains such severe damage to her intestines."

Victims

The female victim was born and raised in Delhi while her parents were from a small village in the Ballia district of Uttar Pradesh. Her father, who sold his agricultural land to educate her, works for a private company as a loader in Delhi.

Complying with Indian law, the real name of the victim was initially not released to the media, so pseudonyms were used for her by various media houses instead, including *Jagruti* ("awareness"), *Amanat* ("treasure"), *Nirbhaya* ("fearless one"), *Damini* ("lightning", after the 1993 Hindi film *Damini*) and Delhi braveheart.

The male victim is 28 years old, from Gorakhpur, Uttar Pradesh, and lives in Ber Sarai, New Delhi.

Delhi police registered a criminal case against the editor of a Delhi based tabloid, *Mail Today*, for disclosing the female victim's identity; as such disclosure is an offence under section 228(A) of Indian Penal Code. Shashi Tharoor, union minister, suggested that if the parents had no objection, her identity could be made public, with a view to showing respect for her courageous response by naming future laws after her, but Tharoor's remark created controversy. Later, her father and brother said that "if her name is made public for this purpose, they have no objection to it" as well as "if the government names the revised anti-rape law after her, they have no objection and it would be an honor to her."

Treatment and death

> On 19 December 2012, the woman underwent her fifth surgery, removing most of her remaining intestine. Doctors reported that she was in "stable but critical" condition. On 21 December, the government appointed a committee of physicians to ensure she received the best medical care.

By 25 December, she remained intubated, on life support and in critical condition. Doctors stated that she was running a fever of 102 degrees to 103 degrees and internal bleeding due to sepsis, a severe blood infection that can lead to organ failure, was somewhat controlled. It was reported that she was "stable, conscious and meaningfully communicative."

At a cabinet meeting chaired by Manmohan Singh on 26 December, the decision was made to fly her to Mount Elizabeth Hospital in Singapore for further care. Mount Elizabeth is a multi-organ transplant specialty hospital.

The decision to move the patient while she was still in critical condition has been criticized for being purely political. Doctors have questioned the need to transfer an <u>intensive care unit</u> (ICU) patient for organ transplants that were not scheduled for weeks or even months later. Government sources indicate that the <u>Chief Minister of Delhi</u>, <u>Sheila Dikshit</u>, was personally behind the decision. Hours earlier, Union Minister <u>P. Chidambaram</u> had stated that the woman was not in a condition to move. Some reports suggest that the decision to shift was taken when it was already clear that she would not survive the next 48 hours.

During the six-hour flight by air-ambulance to Singapore on 27 December, the woman suddenly went into a "near collapse", which a later report described as a cardiac arrest. The doctors on the flight created an arterial line to stabilize her but she had been without pulse and blood pressure for nearly three minutes and never regained consciousness in Singapore.

On 28 December 2012, at 11 am (IST), her condition was "extremely critical" and the chief executive officer of the <u>Mount Elizabeth Hospital</u> said that the woman suffered brain damage, pneumonia, abdominal infection, and that she was "fighting for her life." Her condition continued to deteriorate, and she died at 4:45 am on 29 December, Singapore Standard Time (2:15 am, 29 December, <u>IST</u>; 8:45 pm, 28 December, <u>UTC</u>). Her body was cremated on 30 December 2012 in Delhi under high police security. The government denied access to the media and the public. The "fortification" of Delhi was criticized by many, including the main opposition party of India.

Alleged perpetrators arrested

Police found and arrested some suspects within 24 hours. From recordings made by a highway CCTV vehicle, a description of the bus, a white charter bus with a name written on it, was broadcast. Other operators identified it as being contracted by a South Delhi private school. They then traced it and found its driver, Ram Singh. Police obtained sketches of the assailants with the help of the male victim, and used a cell phone stolen from the two victims to find one of the assailants.

Six men were arrested in connection with the incident. They included Ram Singh, the bus driver, and his brother, Mukesh Singh, who were both arrested in Rajasthan. Vinay Sharma, an assistant gym instructor, and Pawan Gupta, a fruit seller, were both arrested in Delhi. A seventeen year old Raju a juvenile from Badayun, Uttar Pradesh, was arrested at the Anand Vihar terminal in Delhi and Akshay Thakur, who had come to Delhi seeking employment, was arrested in Aurangabad.

According to reports, the group had been eating and drinking together and "having a party" earlier in the day. The juvenile had only met the others that day.

Although the charter bus which Ram Singh drove on weekdays was not permitted to pick up public passengers or even to operate in Delhi because of its tinted windows, they decided to take it out "to have some fun." With Mukesh Singh driving, they first picked up a carpenter who was charged Rs. 10 for a ticket and then robbed of Rs. 8,000 and ejected in South Delhi. They then turned back and a half hour later picked up the couple who were charged Rs. 10 each.

Shortly after the attacks, Gupta said he accepted his guilt and should be hanged. Ram Singh was presented before the Metropolitan Magistrate on 18 December 2012. Mukesh Singh, who was placed in <u>Tihar Jail</u> after his arrest, was assaulted by other inmates and was kept in <u>solitary confinement</u> for his own protection. Ram and Mukesh Singh lived in Ravidas camp, a <u>slum</u> in South Delhi. Ram Singh suffered from a substantial disability in his right arm, sustained after a bus accident for which he had sought compensation. He refused to participate in an identification process.

On 11 March Ram Singh was discovered hanging from a ventilator shaft in his cell about 5.45am. Authorities said it was unclear whether it was a suicide or a murder. It was later reported that Ram Singh was prone to mood swings. His friends called Ram Singh "Mental" alluding perhaps abnormal behavior at times. In 2009, Ram Singh had a serious accident. His wife's death three years ago of kidney failure had added to the rage, said police.

Prosecution

The male victim testified in court on 19 December 2012. The female victim recorded her statement with a sub-divisional magistrate at the Safdarjung Hospital on 21 December, in the presence of the Deputy Commissioner of police.

On 21 December, the government promised to file the <u>charge sheet</u> "quickly" and seek the maximum penalty of life imprisonment for the perpetrators. Following public outrage and a demand for a speedy trial and prosecution, on 24 December the police promised to file the charge sheet within one week. The Parliamentary Standing Committee on Home Affairs met on 27 December to discuss the issue, and Union Home Secretary R. K. Singh and <u>Delhi Police</u> Commissioner Neeraj Kumar were summoned to appear. At the suggestion of the Delhi Chief Minister, the Delhi High Court approved the creation of five fast-track courts to try rape and sexual assault cases. The first of the five approved fast track courts was inaugurated on 2 January 2013 by Altamas Kabir, Chief Justice of India, in Saket court complex of South Delhi. The fast track court will conduct the trial of the accused.

On 21 December 2012, the <u>Delhi High Court</u> reprimanded the Delhi police for being "evasive" in a probe status report providing details of officers on patrol duty in the area covered by the bus route. A further court hearing on the matter was scheduled for 9

January 2013. The following day, the Delhi Police initiated action against three <u>Hauz Khas</u> police station personnel for alleged inaction on an alleged robbery of the bus on which the gang rape and assault occurred. Just before the gang rape, the accused had robbed a carpenter, Ramadhar, after picking him up in their area. On 24 December, two Assistant Commissioners of Police were suspended for failing to prevent the gang rape incident.

On 28 December the victim died from her injuries and five days later, on 3 January 2013, the police filed charges against the five adult men for rape, murder, kidnapping, destruction of evidence, and the attempted murder of the woman's male companion. If convicted, they will be eligible for the death penalty. Senior lawyer Dayan Krishnan has been appointed as the special public prosecutor.

On 9 January, a day before the case was expected to be handed over to the fast-track court for trial; Ram Singh, Mukesh Kumar and Akshay Thakur were planning to plead 'Not Guilty', according to their legal defense team. On 10 January, one suspect's lawyer, Manohar Lal Sharma, announced that his client would plead not guilty to all charges. **Sharma states that the victims are responsible for the assault because they should not have been using public transportation and, as an unmarried couple, they should not have been on the streets at night. In an interview he said, "Until today I have not seen a single incident or**

example of rape with a respected lady. Even an underworld don would not like to touch a girl with respect." He further finds the male victim "wholly responsible" for the incident because he "failed in his duty to protect the woman."

The juvenile, Raju, will be tried separately in a Juvenile court. In the charge sheet the Delhi Police described him as the most brutal of the six accused.[73][74][75] His role is elaborated in the 33-page charge sheet.[76] The accused was declared as 17 years and six months old on the day of the crime by the Juvenile Justice Board (JJB), which relied on his birth certificate and school documents. The JJB rejected a police request for a bone ossification (age determination) test for a positive documentation of his age.

On 28 January, Raju was declared to be a "minor" by the JJB, which would enable him to be released by 4 June 2013, when he attains the age of 18. According to section 16 of The Juvenile Justice (Care and Protection of Children) Act, 2000, a juvenile can only be kept at a reform home till he attains 18 years of age and he cannot be sent to jail thereafter, which in effect would result in his release less than six months after the rape and murder. A petition moved by Janata Party president Subramanian Swamy seeking the prosecution of the juvenile along with the five adults accused in a fast track court because of the ghastly nature of his crime was rejected by the Juvenile Justice Board presided over by Principal Magistrate Geetanjali Goel in New Delhi.

International reaction

The American embassy released a statement on 29 December, offering their condolences to the woman's family and stating "we also recommit ourselves to changing attitudes and ending all forms of gender-based violence, which plagues every country in the world". The United States Government, has granted Nirbhaya "Fearless" the 2013 International Women of Courage Award.

In Paris, people participated in a march to the Indian embassy where a petition was handed over asking for action to make India safer for women.

UN Secretary General Ban Ki-moon issued this statement: "Violence against women must never be accepted, never excused, never tolerated. Every girl and woman has the right to be respected, valued and protected" United Nations Entity for Gender Equality and the Empowerment of Women, who called on the Government of India and the Government of Delhi "to do everything in their power to take up radical reforms, ensure justice and reach out with robust public services to make women's lives more safe and secure."

Demonstrations have also been held in Bangladesh, Pakistan, Nepal and Sri Lanka. The protests there have taken inspiration from the Indian protests, but are also focusing on local issues about rape and domestic violence.

In the wake of remarks against India in western media, Jessica Valenti, writing in *The Nation*, also pointed out that such rapes are common in the United States as well, but US commentators exhibit a double standard in denying or minimizing their systemic nature while simultaneously attacking India for an alleged rape culture. Similar criticisms were aired in *The Massachusetts Daily Collegian*, where commentator Hannah Sparks asserted that the coverage of the Delhi rape case in US media has been more extensive than the Steubenville High School rape case that occurred in the United States in the same year, and that this illustrates the extensive hypocrisy of American media commentators who attack Indians.

Author and activist Eve Ensler, who organized One Billion Rising, a global campaign to end violence against women and girls, said that the gang rape and murder has been a huge turning point in India and around the world. Speaking on Democracy Now Ensler said that "India is really leading the way for the world" in efforts to address violence against women. Ensler said that she had travelled to India at the time of the rape and murder and that after "...having worked every day of my life for the last 15 years on sexual violence, I have never seen anything like that, where sexual violence broke through the consciousness and was on the front page, nine articles in every paper every day, in the center of every discourse, in the center of the college students' discussions, in the center of any restaurant you went in.   And I think what's happened in India, India is really leading the way for the world. It's really broken through. They are actually fast-tracking laws. They are looking at sexual education. **They are looking at the bases of patriarchy and masculinity and how all that leads to sexual violence**."

I used this article as a way to promote understanding of the violence perpetrated against women in places around the world. This article shows an extreme case to be sure, but what it speaks to is the undervaluing of women, the ability for men in this case to claim the incident was the victims fault as well as the woman's companion who failed to protect the woman. Placing blame on the victims has been a habit if you will of many over time.

This article was taken from the internet and is used to help educate the public as set forth Section 107 (the Fair Use Doctrine) of the US Copyright Act of 1976 and is used here for educational purposes to enlighten the public about crimes against women.

"What Terrifies Religious Extremists Like the Taliban Are Not American Tanks or Bombs or Bullets, It's A Girl With A Book"

Malala Yousafzai

Chapter Eleven

EVEN THOUGH I KNEW

I knew better yet still jumped on to my path with both feet. Even that should be a warning, even if you know better and you still choose an abusive relationship thinking that you can "change him" or "save him" this is certainly not the best idea. I think I was the pied piper for years thinking subconsciously that if only he would follow me over this way he would see the light, he would see a better way to have a marriage, he would see my value, understand me, love me, want me, choose me. The list was endless and it kept me very involved in trying to accomplish the good relationship I knew we could have. Except for the part where we could not have that relationship. It did not and never would exist.

I knew from the very beginning that this was not the relationship for me yet I went down this path EVEN THOUGH I KNEW BETTER. Why? Ultimately I think there were many reasons for me, but only two that really explain why. First, I wanted to please my family. I had yet to grow up and mature. I thought they approved of Sam and thought I was nuts to leave him in the beginning of our relationship. I had almost walked away. I also did not want to fail. The next reason and ultimately the reason I stayed so long and did not give up was because I became addicted to the relationship and to the struggle. It was an arm wrestling match about many things. Sam was as locked into this addiction to the relationship as I was. Neither of us wanted to say "Uncle." Obviously we must have been getting something we needed out of the relationship even if it was negative. How can one be addicted to a relationship or to a dynamic that is bad for them and stay in it? It is my opinion from my own experience that part of the abusive relationship is the two partners' addiction to it.

The abuser in my case was always struggling with his need to feel in control and he needed me as a means to that end. I needed to feel connected and understood and so I continually worked for that connection with my abuser. I would say the need to get my partner to really understand me was what drove me the most. I thought he had me all wrong, he just didn't get me or my real motivations, but once he did all would be well. The all-encompassing and total need for my mates understanding was what I worked for much like an addict on Facebook who needs the likes he or she finds waiting for them after they have torn themselves away from it the night before. My abuser was in this wrestling match with me so that he could stay on top, to feel power and control over me and our family.

It seems obvious to anyone reading this that this was a lose, lose situation. Don't forget that this was what felt "normal" to me. If I could just work this out I could be happy and live the life I wanted with this man that I loved. How could he not see it? How could he not understand it? How could he not meet me in the middle or somewhere? If only became my thought pattern. If only he could see, hear, know, feel, love, understand, get it, if only he would talk to me, connect with me, if only, if only, if only. My entire world eventually revolved around working for this connection.

His whole world revolved in making sure we did not achieve this connection. Like two magnets with the wrong ends pointed towards each other we were never to meet in the middle. This must be what they meant when they say polar opposites. But, you have to give us an A++ for trying to connect or not connect depending on which side you are on. (Get it?) Levity is good for the soul. I would say that part of what saved me was and is my sense of humor. Looking back now I have to laugh at my sheer determination and stubbornness at not giving up sooner and I also cried many, many tears for the same thing. I lost so much time and had so much pain because of it. But, boy did I learn these lessons down to my soul. The lessons about myself and why I had to travel this road brought me here and I am glad to be here. The lessons though are imprinted in my cells, my layers of me from the very core of me to the outside layers. Probably one of the hardest things I have ever done up to this moment was to slowly, inch by inch, piece by piece dismantle and take apart my connection and my addiction to this relationship.

Even after being separated three years and wanting for this to be over, knowing that I needed to let go and move on I still had fleeting thoughts about should I stay, it's all I know, I love him, he needs me things like that. I know better, I knew better yet I still thought he was the devil I knew. I was afraid to move on afraid I would not find the love I deserved out there in the abyss. This man was all I knew in every sense of the word. I still wanted to run back for a moment to what was familiar and what was "normal" even though it was the absolute worst thing I could possibly do. This is why women who are battered physically go home with their abusers. Because our self-esteem is so battered from abuse whether physical, verbal or both we become addicted to what we know even if eventually it isn't really safe. We have so many reasons to stay and so many fears about the unknown. There is fear whether we stay or whether we contemplate going.

I knew finally that this had been an addiction when after the end was finally near and the death of our relationship was imminent I had the thought "Maybe I am making a mistake, maybe I should stay." I repeat this statement because it was almost a physical pull much like an addiction to substances or gambling have. It was like trying to shed a worn out shoe that you can no longer wear, but it was familiar and in many ways comfortable. Maybe it even hurt your feet to wear, but I was almost willing for a split second to overlook it. Whew! I did not go back for more. In this way it really

is an addiction to what is known and the fear about
how to live in and with different choices.

Chapter 12
Subjugation

I found this an important reminder of the scope of this words definition

Synonyms

dominate, overpower, pacify, subdue, subject, conquer, subordinate, vanquish

Related Words

annihilate, beat, clobber, crush, defeat, drub, lick, mow (down), overcome, prevail (over), reduce, rout, skunk, smash, thrash, triumph (over), trounce, wallop, whip; enslave; break, clamp down (on), crack down (on), put down, quash, quell, repress, silence, smother, snuff (out), squash, squelch, suppress

Subjugation is a state of being under control or secondary.

When a culture keeps women inferior to men and doesn't let them advance, this is an example of subjugation.

Subjugation is like oppression or conquest: one group takes control over another and forces them to do as they're told.

Subjugation is one of many types of injustice in the world.   It has to do with one group of people dominating another group by taking away their freedom. When slavery was legal in the U.S. that was a clear-cut case of subjugation: African-Americans were forced to live without rights, under the control of their white owners. To remember this word, think of its Latin root *subjugat,* which means "brought under a yoke."

DEFINITIONS OF: subjugation1

forced submission to control by others

> <u>repression</u>
> a state of forcible subjugation
> <u>oppression</u>
> the state of being kept down by unjust use of force or authority: "after years of oppression they finally revolted"
> <u>captivity,</u> <u>enslavement</u>
> the state of being a slave
> <u>bondage,</u> <u>slavery,</u> <u>thralldom,</u> <u>thrall,</u> <u>thralldom</u>
> the state of being under the control of another person
> <u>bondage</u>
> the state of being under the control of a force or influence or abstract power
> <u>confinement</u>
> the state of being confined
> <u>yoke</u>
> an oppressive power
> <u>servitude</u>

state of subjection to an owner or master or forced labor imposed as punishment

the act of conquering

Synonyms:
conquering, conquest, subjection

the act of subjugating by cruelty

Synonyms:
oppression
Type of:
persecution
the act of persecuting (especially on the basis of race or religion)

- All those conditions--economic dysfunction, illiteracy, female **subjugation**--still exist.

I felt it important to include the definition of subjugation as noted by Wikipedia and other sources because even if those of us over a certain age may not have forgotten the words or their definition, I am afraid that the generations that follow us don't know and won't know what women have fought for when it comes to gender equality in the last 50 years. Current young women may not know about the struggles faced by women in our country from the beginning of time.

For example, I went back to college at the age of 52 taking Gender classes, Psychology of Aging (Ageism) and every Psych and Sociology class I could get my hands on. Unless a young woman takes Women's Studies Classes and Women's History they won't hear and won't know when women gained the right to vote, Roe Vs Wade, how a woman could not file her own patent, own her own property, get a bank account or credit in her own name without a husband's permission, the list goes on. One really needs to not only want to learn about women's history they have to take an active role in discovering where they, where we came from. It should be required just as studies on men in our history is.

In 1960's America it was a common practice that if a woman was ill or even terminal to discuss protocol's or treatment options with a husband rather than the woman herself to determine what to do. To treat or not to treat. There were times when the woman herself would not even be told all of the details or all of the options for her own well-being. This is what happened to Rachel Carson an author and female scientist and human being that is one of my most cherished authors and persons. When Rachel received the diagnosis of cancer and did go through treatment, when it returned and because she had NO husband the doctor's left Ms. Carson out of the equation never telling her anything about treatment options. They let the cancer advance without telling her or informing her enough to take advantage of anything in order to save or prolong her life.

Rachel Carson first began writing articles and used her initials knowing that if the people who read her papers and scientific information that she would be taken more seriously if people thought she was a man. While she was dying she painstakingly wrote a classic novel called Silent Spring, a book that would launch the environmental movement.

I am concerned that there may not be much dialog about women's issues between younger women. They don't know a different world where women did not work, a man could force his wife to have sex without consequence, and there were no such words as sexual harassment in the work place because if it was occurring it was shielded under the conspiracy of silence I talked about in chapter ten.

Women still earn less for the same job a man holds. I say to you, REALLY? As I have looked around I am worried at the apathy or complacency that it seems I am witnessing in the next generations. I am talking about two generations that follow me. Women aged 18 to 30 seem to be less aware of the struggle their own gender has had over time and that is because it is not widely taught. Or... if they have heard the history they have not really understood that there is still much to be done.   Women in American Culture classes even Women's History classes are not taught to us and if they are and if there are those who get it and get involved I am wondering where the younger generations outrage and passion are. I say this because I have recently been in college myself. I have been the oldest woman in the room.

In discussions in different sociology classes I have taken, psychology classes I have taken I have been shocked that none of these young women vote in elections. Recently in my class in Popular Culture there was discussion about politics where the subject of voting came up. The class was about evenly divided between men and women. I was told specifically that maybe forty something percent of people in general vote (the number is supposed to actually be about 58%), and the men in the class tried to argue the case about why it does not matter if they vote. This one gentleman said their vote did not really matter and the system was broken anyway. I told him that this was the only thing he had to voice any opinion about anything that is going on within his own government.

I told him even if in a presidential election enough people checked the box None of the above that at least he would be, and they would be making a statement about the government and the political mess that the elections have turned out to be. My next statement was this, "Oh I forgot as a Caucasian man who has never not had the right to vote, you probably are taking that right for granted. Women did not get the right to vote until fifty years after the black man in 1920." 1920! Even after the slaves were freed and the black MAN was granted the right to vote the word sex was left out of the amendment to the constitution granting women the right to vote. There were women at that time asking for the right to vote and inclusion to the amendment but they were ignored. Women had to fight for this right for another fifty years. I of course think that it was ridiculous to be left out of this amendment. The right to vote is in my opinion a human right and the inequality of women is a human rights issue, a civil rights issue and equality is simply the right, just and correct way to look at this issue.

All of the old ways to view women as less than, property, less intelligent, second class citizens, someone to control or have power over, should be gone by now yet they are ever more prevalent in today's society. If all women that exist at this moment in the United States of America used their right to vote to be heard there would be no denying our collective voices. I say to all of you reading this please do not let this issue sit for the next fifty years. We do not have time to waste. Women as a strong united voice can make a difference and make a positive change for women in their community, in the classroom, in the workplace and in the home and in the world. Education of men about human rights, education of women about their worth and their rights is something that can be done and should be done. The United States of America historically over time has told all of us inaccurate stories about what has happened in our past.

For example, in addition to the glaring injustice of slavery, the treatment of Native Americans from the moment Europeans got to this land up to this moment was told with a slant as though the Native Americans were the bad guys. We know of course that this is not and was not true. Americans have historically tried to make us sound as though we are always on the side of right and that we are most likely really the good guys in conflicts. Even the story of Christopher Columbus was told to us as children as though he was the best guy in the world having discovered America. This is of course an inaccurate portrayal of the man and of history. My point is that the story and stories we tell ourselves as a nation that we believe in equality, we support equality of all kinds that the reality is that it takes a very long time in our society to actually stand up for what is right and what is good. Women have long been the subject that is not mentioned but by a few. I don't know if people are apathetic or if everyone thinks the status quo of today is good enough.

While I am on this particular rant about history let me say that our history books have been inaccurate about women who have contributed to our nation and that even when it comes to inventions and contributions made by women the whole and accurate truth has not been told or taught. Men are listed as the inventors of things because women and black people, slaves were not allowed to hold patents and so men were given the credit in our history books and on the patents. Women were not allowed to own property. If a woman's husband died many times the oldest son would inherit everything with the widow not able to own property.

There was no such thing as a community property state either. I think it is so important to study about women and women in American History. We are now forced to take as a requirement to graduate in college classes that are designed to make us more culturally sensitive when it comes to race and ethnicity. But nowhere is it a requirement to address women's issues and educate not only women but men on these issues. Men have always taken it for granted that they have all rights and there is a certain arrogance that comes with that. It is taken for granted because all of their rights have been there always. There was no fight for equality. The power structure, hierarchy is set up the same way it always was. Think about it. If you are a white, (Caucasian) man in the United States of America more doors are open to you automatically as a sort of birthright. If you are a man of any color or ethnicity you come next, then women of every color.

Why discuss these issues in a book about verbal abuse? Because the way the system has been set up, the way we are taught as women what our roles are or should be is how we ourselves as women get the idea that it is ok to be treated as second class or less than men. If we are taught this then it becomes very confusing and very difficult for some of us to stand up, realize that it is NOT OK to be talked down to, patronized, condescended to and discounted. It is NOT OK to be verbally or physically abused. This is not part of the job description as some would have us believe. For me it is this simple. If women are taught that we have to take it, put up with it and if we actually expect to be treated this way in our society it must be "NORMAL?"

This is why it is important to teach your female children that it is NOT NORMAL, is not part of what we must take or put up with. We must teach our children what appropriate behavior is when it comes from men and then to choose not to be around men or anyone who treats us inappropriately. It is a battle in today's society because of the stereotypes that exist and prevail. That is why I complain about media, commercials, and the sex sells mentality. Have we not moved past the stage in our history where men sit on couches hoping to visually see T & A roll by while trying to sell them beer, cheeseburgers and just about anything else? Who of these men or women for that matter will actually be buying bras and underwear from these childlike looking skinny girls just past puberty really? Will you be going there? Will your husband, son or boyfriend, next door neighbor be going there to try to figure out what size bra or underwear will squeeze your T & A into them?

I say enough already. It is no longer ok. We collectively as women do not share a loud enough voice in asking for it to stop. The young girls of today must suffer greatly because of what the media tells them it is ok to be. If our obesity rates are skyrocketing yet we are shown constantly that we must be young, pretty, skinny and be shaped a certain way. Shame on our society for teaching this. I know there are groups and organizations out there that are fighting the good fight and trying to stop the messages our girls receive, trying to tell young girls it is ok to be who and how they are.

It is ok to love yourself and that you have wonderful qualities like a great brain, a sense of humor, empathy and caring for others and to be ok with the shape of your body, your face, your nose, you name it. And most importantly the real ability to do ANYTHING and EVERYTHING we choose to be and do.

Consciously I think it's possible that many women of today may believe in many ways our battle for equality has been won. This issue is important because subconsciously and in many ways consciously our society still tells us this is not true. I talk about these issues because until men are taught, believe and act as though they do not have the right to verbally abuse and then physically abuse women we have not won the battle. Until we as women do not put up with the status quo, taking abuse, not telling and talking about it and as long as there remains a conspiracy of silence there will continue to be power and control over women by men and the subjugation of women will continue being allowed by both women and men.

Women have to be as usual, and as always the ones who seek change in a real way and then make it happen. This is and has always been true. Any change in any family starts with women and then the family follows. Think about it. Any time a woman has decided to help her family eat better, sleep earlier, conserve energy, shop at certain stores and places, any change within a family that typically has to do with being better usually comes from or is instigated by a woman. I am certain this statement may make some men a bit irritated with me, but statistically and in reality I think the facts do bear this out. Domestic violence will not end and will only get worse over time until we ask for change and are willing to do the work to make the changes we want and deserve happen.

Education from the moment we as humans get here is the key. Our society has not caught up with the fact that women and girls are human beings just as their male counterparts are. Women are as smart and as capable as the rest of the human race. The Constitution was written with the words, "We the People", but at the time what they did not say but effectively really did say was "We the White Men in the United States of America." Minorities, Native Americans, Black Americans and Women of all races were not really who they were talking about. I apologize if this offends anyone, I am expressing how I see it. Later amendments to the constitution were added to make others feel equal but this did not happen without a fight as we all know. Real equality for all of the groups who were not initially included in the Constitution did not happen for another 100 to 150 years. "We The People" (minorities) Gay Americans and Women are all still fighting for true equality as I write this and it is 2018.

I cannot be the only HUMAN in America who cringes almost every time people in politics, the news media and in too many places to count, the words that are used have the word men included instead of the word humans, people or other non-gender specific words. In the 1970's there was an uproar enough so that in articles, stories, and speaking women called attention to the fact that we were left out in general. Stories in school always mentioned "he" never "she." Now we have had many changes to stories and to written speeches and messages. Yet, still when politicians and many public speakers still say only the word men it bothers me. At this juncture in time I would change every old spoken message to the American People to include the word human people – or men and women not just men. This one simple change could and would lead the way for the rest of society, the world to think about all people, all humans not just men. It is such a subtle thing, but something that I am certain no men truly spend time thinking about because they are and always have been included. They have always been the subject of many a speech. The Constitution of the United States is about men, free white men. It is time to be included in every way and in everything as equals. Women are people, humans, with voices.

Chapter 13
Human Rights

The basic rights and freedoms, to which all humans are entitled, often held to include the right to life and liberty, freedom of thought and expression, and equality before the law.

The American Heritage® Dictionary of the English Language,

Fourth Edition copyright ©2000 by Houghton Mifflin Company.

Updated in 2009. Published by Houghton Mifflin Company. All rights reserved.

There are so many who have never known about our rights and that they encompass so much. I had to include them here.

1. We are **all born free and equal**

2. Don't discriminate

3. The Right to life

4. No slavery

5. No torture

6. You have Rights no matter where you go

7. We're **all equal before the law**

8. Your human rights are protected by law

9. No unfair detainment

10. The Right to trial

11. We're always innocent until proven guilty

12. The Right to privacy

13. The freedom to move

14. The Right to asylum

15. Right to a Nationality

16. Marriage and Family

17. The Right to Ownership

18. Freedom of Thought

19. Freedom of expression

20. The Right to public assembly

21. The Right to Democracy

22. Social Security

23. Worker's Rights

24. The Right to play

25. Food and Shelter for All

30. No One Can Take Away Your Human Rights

There is much more detail explaining what exactly is meant by each right listed in The Story of Human Rights.

These Human Rights are documented and can be found here:

humanrights.com and info@humanrights.com

"Where, after all, do universal human rights begin? In small places, close to home – so close and so small that they cannot be seen on any maps of the world. Yet they are the world of the individual person; the neighborhood he lives in; the school or college he attends; the factory, farm, or office where he works. Such are the places where every man, woman and child seeks equal justice, equal opportunity, equal dignity without discrimination. Unless these rights have meaning there, they have little meaning anywhere. Without concerted citizen action to uphold them close to home, we shall look in vain for progress in the larger world." - Eleanor Roosevelt

I recommend reading in detail each article in the Universal Declaration of Human Rights. An estimated

90 percent of us are unable to name more than three of our thirty rights.

A very simple quote I heard a few years ago is this: "Feminism is the radical notion that women are people." It really is that simple, at least for me. For people (women) of today feminism should not be a scary word. Stigma has been attached to the word and to the woman who claims to be a feminist of today. In the 70's women were proud to call themselves feminists'. We were making strides in voicing how wrong it is to be treated as and labeled second class citizens. If you claim to be a feminist now and you are active at living as an example of a strong woman who believes in herself and others, a woman who cares enough to work for women's causes and equality, to make the world a better place for the future of our daughters and their daughters, how can feminism be a scary word? Claim it and work with it and yes fight for it. Equality and humanity is all that this is. I cannot believe that logic and reason will not prevail in the 21st century.

I will say it again, "Feminism is the radical notion that women are people." I might change it a bit to say "Feminism is the radical notion that women are human people of equal value." Gay men and women are very vocal, fighting hard for equal rights under the law to be married to each other, to be able to inherit, to be buried next to one another, to be treated as equal human beings under the law. Little by little they are fighting to break down our society's moral judgments and stigma, stereotypes about them as being less than all of the rest of society. I know there are tons of women out there fighting the good fight and you hear reports from here and there about women's issues. Women in this country fight to help women and girls in other countries every day. Women and girls are gaining more access to an education in many more places around the world than they ever have. There are gains in health care and safety everywhere. I support all of these things. I am grateful for all of the hard work by millions of men and women everywhere in their endeavors.

I am only saying to you this, where is the collective sound of all of our voices in this country, the United States of America when it comes to passing the Equal Rights Amendment once and for all? (I wrote this in 2013) When will I hear and when will we hear women standing up and voicing their opinions on the negative messages shown to us in the media every day? When will we join together again and show the world that we mean what we say about equality? When will we stop letting the status quo stall us losing our momentum?

I think the time is now to move and let America know that in the 21st century it is a shame to continue to blow smoke up our collective you know what's and time to get real about equality, human rights and civil rights once and for all. That reminds me of the flag salute. I pledge allegiance to the flag of the United

States of America and to the Republic for which it stands, one nation under God indivisible with Liberty and Justice for all. For ALL. Hmmmm. The optimistic me is happy with the fact that some progress has been made, but not the speed with which we move to make certain that everyone is treated fairly, equally and with respect. There is also a part of me that is sad about the very idea that we are still stuck and I mean stuck with old gender stereotypes. How long will this and must this go on?

Women or at least most women in my opinion don't plan on giving up themselves when they decide to get married or get married and have children. How many of us want husbands and children as a way of enhancing our lives not diminishing it by letting this choice slowly take away our choices as humans? In many instances and in many families today there is a huge disparity in the division of labor in the family. When a woman works outside the home and has children and has a husband the female is the one that everything seems to fall to in the managing of the home, in managing the children and all of their needs. This is such a huge juggling act. It is no wonder that many women simply do not find the time to take care of themselves.

When women get home from work there are chores needing attention. Even if the children are taught to do their share there are so many other "jobs" that women do after 5. The driving of children even to and from school, events and even the most basic things are **time** demanding. If a woman ever wants to have time to herself or time to do the things that she may have slowly started to forget she enjoyed there is rarely much real time to do them. If there is time the woman can be too tired to make the effort for herself. This is not something that anyone of us plans and our families don't really intentionally do to us. Things like this happen over time because the "mom" is who the family looks to for stability, consistency, and a pair of socks and so on. It is possible that many of us think that this is our job description and who else will do the many tasks of a mom anyway? How can this change for women? Maybe these issues are less of a problem when the family dynamic consists of mostly females as in mom and daughters. This is not a dynamic I am familiar with. In our family and extended family there have mostly been boys. Because of the shortage of women in my family I think it is very possible that in this dynamic the second shift is a lone profession. I believe this stretching of time and the second shift that women are involved in is universal. I do not believe it matters on which continent and in which language you speak. These roles were once extremely useful in the survival of the family. The roles are in need of an overhaul and people, both men and women are in need of exploring new ways to "do" family.

Is the real partnership and the division of labor within families something we can change or foster by educating the men in our lives to pick up more of the day to day work? Making dinner, doing the dishes, laundry, cleaning the toilet, planning schedules and logistics and travel and the list goes on. For those of you ladies who have enough funding to pay for all of these jobs to be done by someone else more power to you. But, for those of the rest of us who must manage everything with little help we end up feeling like there is never enough time or energy to accomplish any of the tasks assigned well.

Forget being able to nourish ourselves by taking a class, reading a book or learning something we always wanted to. Yes, we signed up for this without full knowledge of the real job description. I personally am very glad I only had two children. They are thirteen years apart in age so in effect it was like having two only children. Even this in addition to running my own business and running a home could occasionally be overwhelming. Squeezing in things I enjoy has been interesting to say the least. It would not matter if I had more than one lifetime to fit "me" into the equation and to take better care of "my needs." Then I would not feel as pressured as the clock ticks towards time out.

The clock is ticking and each generation of women has made strides in the quest for equality. But! why am I still talking about this, why are many women of my age asking what has happened to real equality? The kind that has been achieved so that there is no longer the need for voicing it, fighting for it and telling the world that what still goes on today across the globe in trying to keep power and control over women is WRONG?

Human RIGHTS, Civil RIGHTS and Equal RIGHTS … that is all I am talking about.

Chapter 14
Bits and Pieces about discrimination against women

When I started college and took a class called Women in American Culture it was 1975. I had graduated early from high school, starting college having just barely turned 17. The world was changing it seemed, rapidly. Women's causes were being pushed to the forefront. I had wanted to possibly become a social worker and to help somehow in our society. At 20 I was happy with the progress women appeared to be making. We had the pill; we were working outside the home. We told the world we would not be defined by the skirt we wore. I wore pant suits and when I felt really rowdy I would wear a tie with my shirt to make a statement to the world of men I encountered on the job every day.

The trouble is I was about to discover sexual harassment on the job was to be quietly taken if you wanted to keep your job. You had to suck it up and not discuss it with anyone or you would not be able to pay the rent. It made me angry that I was either to take it or if I complained I would lose my job. I wanted my job. It was the beginning of my career in Computer Installation. I was there in the beginning of the computer age. I should not have had to try and figure out at the age of 21 how to juggle trying to be nice to the boss who was married already and how to not compromise myself. What woman has ever wanted to juggle a career choice with not making the boss mad?

So, in 2009 as I reentered college and began to pursue a degree in earnest I knew what the last thirty-five years had taught me. Things had not changed enough and some things had reverted back to before the women's movement.

The following perspectives came from papers I wrote in classes in Psychology and Sociology. I felt it important to share them here. In every class I could possibly share with men, women, younger women and men I talked about women's issues. The papers are partly based on my own opinions as well as facts reported by many various sources who I have rightly given credit to. If you find them repetitive it is because I borrowed from my own book here and there when I wrote my papers or vice versa. Reminders can be a good thing.

At the end of this book in addition to the bibliography and credits for sources I have added a list of book recommendations if you are interested in reading more about perspectives on women over time as well as taking a trip through history (not long ago history) of women who helped moved women forward in their own way.

Keep in mind if you choose to read Freidan's "The Feminine Mystic" when you get to the statement that many women were suffering from the problem that has no name, I might add that in addition to women's discrimination in general which defines and names the problems that women face that women were routinely getting wonderful educations and then often (mostly always) asked to stay home and provide a home for a man. In so doing there were many who wanted more. They wanted to use their talents. Prior to the signing into law the Equal Opportunities laws in the 1960's there was not only widespread discrimination in the workplace, but ads of the times were placed under headings that read FEMALE and MALE. A woman could not expect an interview for a job under the men's column. Sad to say that although the laws had been signed in the 1960's when I began looking for work in the 1970's this practice was still being done. I distinctly recall those same headings as I searched newspaper ads for a job at that time. This was the late 1970's. Time needed to be up then. 42 years later is it?

Laurie Ault
Sociology 114 Gender
Project Topic
November 4, 2012

The historical context of the discrimination of women

Comparison to racial discrimination for black and women men during civil rights

I would like to talk a bit about historical perspective when it comes to American Women and the changes that have occurred over time from the right to vote in 1921 to the 1950's, 1960's and 1970's highlighting the important issues. I want to discuss the women's movement and the gains made that were and are real versus what is only a façade for change or "blowing smoke" so to speak. The comparison can include how things are now and the question have we gone backward in the last 40 years since Roe versus Wade?

I mention in my title the comparison for women and equal rights to racial discrimination for black society from slavery to civil rights and to current times because I believe there is a correlation in the way it feels to be a woman throughout time and currently. The difference is that black men have made more real strides over time than women of any nationality or ethnic identity from any country including the United States of America.

Inequality of Women

1878 the first suffrage
amendment was presented
to Congress &
reintroduced every year
for **40 years** but was
never voted on

Women were the last citizens of the United States to be afforded FULL citizenship under the constitution, after the black man. It took 72 years spanning two centuries, 18 presidencies and three wars for women to achieve the right to vote.

The Nineteenth Amendment

The right of citizens of the United States to vote shall not be denied or abridged by the United States or by any State on account of sex. Congress shall have the power to enforce this article by appropriate legislation. Ratified August 18, 1920.

The Fifteenth Amendment

- The **Fifteenth Amendment** (**Amendment XV**) to the United States Constitution prohibits each government in the United States from denying a citizen the right to vote based on that citizen's "race, color, or previous condition of servitude" (for example, slavery). It was ratified on February 3, 1870. Please note that the word Sex was omitted resulting in a 50 year delay in women's right to vote.

The Nineteenth Amendment

- The right of citizens of the United States to vote shall not be denied or abridged by the United States or by any State on account of sex. Congress shall have the power to enforce this article by appropriate legislation
- Ratified August 18, 1920

Gender Roles in society 1950's

- We may have the right to vote, but we are still seen as a compliment to a man, a server, nurturer, mother, not equal
- Less Than Men – inferior brains

Gender Roles in society 1950's
Where's My Dinner?

We may have the right to vote, but we are still seen as a complement to a man, a server, a nurturer, mother, not equal. Husband helper if one has a husband. Less than men and seen as having inferior brains. No really.

Women achieved the right to vote in 1920 – less than 100 years ago

- Woodrow Wilson Quotes about democracy
- "I believe in democracy because it releases the energies of every human being"
- "America is not a mere body of traders; it is a body of free men. Our greatness built upon freedom is moral, not material. We have a great ardor for gain; but we have a deep passion for the rights of man". 1911 New York
- Alice Paul was instrumental in fighting for Women's right to vote. She said, in 1972: I never doubted that equal rights was the right direction. Most reforms, most problems are complicated. But to me there is nothing complicated about ordinary equality.

Women achieved the right to vote in 1920 – less than 100 years ago. Woodrow Wilson Quotes about democracy:

"I believe in democracy because it releases the energies of every human being." "America is not a mere body of traders; it is a body of free men. Our greatness built upon freedom is moral, not material. We have a great ardor for gain; but we have a deep passion for the rights of man." 1911 New York

Note the continued omission of the words men and women or mentioning women at all.

Alice Paul was instrumental in fighting for Women's right to vote. She said in 1972: "I never doubted that equal rights was the right direction. Most reforms, most problems are complicated. But to me there is nothing complicated about ordinary equality."

Discrimination against any group is still discrimination

- Mississippi A Self Portrait
- Booker Wright
  http://youtu.be/W1lUQ0fgrFY?t=11m28s
- The justification of treating people as though they are less than
- Who was in charge? Who is still in charge? Of the media, what we see as normal. Who prescribes how we treat each other?
- What do they have to gain by perpetuating the stories they tell and want us to see?

Sociology Script I wrote:

In the 1960's the civil rights movement helped to end or at least make it more of a taboo to be an outright bigot. Civil rights should have meant equal rights for all people, all humans. Yet, half the populations of the planet earth are being omitted. This interesting omission in history is the omission of women and their many contributions in our history and in our culture no matter what color. Native Americans, blacks and white women all are not mentioned or are barely, quietly mentioned throughout history. Many types of discrimination against people of color (Black men and women) Ethnic groups, homosexuals, religious groups are all in the forefront when it comes to taboos in our society about saying out loud derogatory statements and generalizations about these groups. However, it is more than ok in 2012 to make any type of comment against women of any color from any ethnic group.

Because I believe mostly in conflict theory as the way our society works (or doesn't work) It makes sense to me that people who have power and control over others want to keep it. Also, competition for scarce resources causes conflict in our society. If wealthy white men are the keepers of power and control and resources in our society, it isn't surprising they want to keep it. They have power over all who have less including women. By keeping the status quo as it is, they have effectively kept power and control over 51% of the population in this country. Over the years' concessions have been made to pacify and contain us by finally accepting that women had to be recognized as full citizens of the United States by being allowed the right to vote. This came with a very nasty fight where women were imprisoned for obstructing traffic in front of the white house. Their civil rights were trampled. Eventually the charges were cleaned from the women's records.

The inclusion or right to vote came more than 50 years after black men. Have you ever wondered why this is so? The fifteenth amendment providing (BLACK MEN) The right to vote could have easily included the word sex after race and color. I especially like: Or previous condition of servitude because the way I see it the condition of servitude for women still exists today. Not just in developing countries, but in our country as well.

I added this in February 2018

And so ultimately, what it came down to was that "women's suffrage in the United States was achieved gradually, at state and local levels during the late 19th century and early 20th century, culminating in 1920 with the passage of the Nineteenth Amendment to the United States Constitution, which provided: "The right of citizens of the United States to vote shall not be denied or abridged by the United States or by any State on account of sex."

Social Problems - Sociology 103

Jensen Jeung, Instructor

March 27, 2014

Inequalities of Gender and Sexual Orientation

The inequality of women has long been an issue that concerns me. I chose this topic because I am a woman and I have a frame of reference about the subject of discrimination based solely on what sex I happen to be. Personally I come from a family full of boys. I am the middle child between two brothers. From the first moments I can remember I was aware of the difference and the preference for the gender that I wasn't. The closest thing I can compare being a female in our society and in the world to is racial discrimination. I think that the reasons gender discrimination still exist today are old outdated ideas about the patriarchal system. Men who have never faced discrimination, or maybe I should say white men, have no idea typically what it is like to be discriminated against based solely on the color of their skin, the ethnicity they happen to be or because of the absence or presence of a particular body part. It is my opinion that during the waves of feminism that moved through time and the progress that was made were times when our society, in particular women saw the discrimination of women as a sociological problem.

It may be that many still feel this way, but the importance of the problems associated with gender discrimination seems to wax and wane over time. The truth is that this is a major sociological problem not only to women but to every society and every system that is set up on this planet. The waste of human potential for half of the world is astounding. In third world countries keeping women in a subjugated system with no education and no self-worth wastes resources that these countries typically do not have the luxury to waste. Because of outdated views and because many times men are not educated about doing life differently with a woman as a partner it has not occurred to men that this could be a change that they might desire. Because the men are also uneducated and because their belief systems are antiquated about the value of women they continue to pass down a solely patriarchal system where women are property, have no rights and are often sold, raped, beaten and even killed. These are not just my opinions they are based in fact as we read in our text. The very first story in our chapter about this issue talks about the problem in Sociological Perspective.

> "You can see how important the sex of a child is in India. Parents living in poverty feel despair at the birth of a girl. "It's like watering someone else's plant" they say. They must feed and clothe her, but she can contribute practically nothing to the family income. Then she marries, and they have to pay a dowry. But the birth of a

boy? The parents rejoice at this. A boy will grow into a man who can help sustain them in old age. (Henslin Page 263)

This way of thinking and teaching generation after generation is the very reason girls are not valued in India's society. This is a self-fulfilling prophecy and will come to pass because of the way girls are treated and not allowed to do anything different. This perspective could have been from last week or one hundred years ago. The only way to change things for the better in countries like India, China and many others is to educate the men and the women about how to make changes to their basic belief systems. Infanticide should be a crime and if the parents do not want a child it should also be a crime to endanger the lives of these babies by uncaring parents who would rather withhold care to see the child die than to be responsible for a female child. This is 2014 not the dark ages.

A current sociological problem that is global is the sex trafficking and slavery going on in virtually every country including the United States of America.

Globally women are disappearing having been kidnapped and sold, being forced into the sex trade with enslaving village girls for the same reason that people got away with enslaving blacks two hundred years ago: The victims are perceived as discounted humans.   "In the 1780's, an average of just under eighty thousand slaves were shipped annually across the Atlantic from Africa to the New World. ""Modern global slave trade is larger in absolute terms than the Atlantic slave trade in the eighteenth and nineteenth centuries was." (Kristof, Nicholas D. Sheryl WuDunn Page 10, 11). What drives sex trafficking is the demand for it.

"Name any country in the world and somewhere a John is purchasing a sex act." (Zuniga Page 12) "He is one of the major players driving the demand for women and girls trafficked into prostitution and sexual exploitation". (Zuniga Page 12) As with other forms of trafficking, sex trafficking is a triangle of activity – supply, demand and distribution says Laura J. Lederer, the U.S. Department of State. (www.state.gov/g/tip/).

One cannot stop the supply and distribution part of the equation and think that will stop trafficking. The demand side of the equation has got to be stopped as well. In just another affront to the human rights of women people know this goes on everywhere but seem satisfied to look the other way. (Conspiracy of Silence).

Many of the players in the equation are women themselves who most likely want the money it brings them. Women own and run the brothels and also hurt, beat and get rid of trouble makers if necessary. Many indignities are forced on the women including murder and disfigurement. Much like the indignities suffered by African Americans and Africans two hundred years ago, globally women still face uncertainty, less rights as humans, violence and the threat of violence every day. Many women who have been assaulted even in this country deal with Post Traumatic Stress Disorders and the worry that comes with having daughters and granddaughters. The incidence of harm to female children and female teens is much higher than boys and men and is usually perpetrated by men.

For example, "one in five girls and one in twenty boys is a victim of child sexual abuse. Twenty percent of adult females and five to ten percent of adult males recall a childhood sexual assault or sexual abuse incident". (National Center for Victims of Crime) http://www.victimsofcrime.org/media/reporting-on-child-sexual-abuse/child-sexual-abuse-...

The overall health of women and girls was all but ignored over time. In yet another area of life the discrepancy and progress in health issues for men and women shows a favor of men's health studies over women's. If there were any studies at all about the effects of medicines on women versus men, they were and are few and far between. As recently as 2008 it was all too obvious there has been a lack of studies with women. Men and women are hormonally different and respond to medicines differently than men. Yet in heart studies although women die of heart disease at the same rate as men do women were absent from clinical trials on the use of aspirin. The studies done were on 35,000 subjects, all men. "The results of the aspirin studies could not be generalized to women because hormonal differences between men and women were not studied. Women receive less aggressive cardiac care, are more likely to die in the hospital, and have greater risk of death from a second heart attack in the year following the first heart attack than men" "Slowly the women's health movement has challenged androcentric medicine by calling attention to the lack of females used in health-related clinical trials, by empowering women as patients, and encouraging them to become practitioners, practices that benefit men as well." (Lindsey Page 53).

In every area of life that has been a challenge for women, education, health, pay inequities, you name it, changes have and are being made to improve the situations of women worldwide. There are solutions to these problems for women and their children. The key is education, not only for women but for men especially in third world countries. In most instances, if a man is educated he will learn he has choices in how to live. He has choices in how he treats himself and others. Old scripts and stereotypes are not working for him or for women. Men need to be taught that women are people and of equal value. This is not happening fast enough anywhere. With the grim story I have just told and the astounding statistics and data that back up this huge story of inequality in many ways it could be seen as hopeless. It is not hopeless. This story needs to be told to make more people aware of the problems. Then movement forward can be made into working with solutions already in place and in finding new strategies to move into the twenty first century.

The United States of America woke up during the times of the enslavement of black people. The abolitionists stepped up to tell everyone that slavery was wrong. A lot of people had looked the other way in this country over the plight of the black slaves saying and thinking that it was just something they had to accept even if they did not like it. Fortunately, there were men and women, black and white who worked hard to abolish slavery telling everyone that it was wrong. It took a fight and it took educating people and changing their minds.

Societies can be convinced to do the right thing when they have had their attentions called to problems and then attention is paid to solving those problems. There is no way we can have the men in this world walk a mile in a woman's shoes. That is typically too funny to see. Much like it is not something we can know about when we try to describe what it feels like to be discriminated against because of the color of our skin, or how we look, if we are short or tall. Women cannot describe to a man and have him feel what it is like to live in the body of a female and to walk in the world every day being treated differently because of how they look. How can one describe to a white man for example what it is like to be a black man? It is no different to be female and to try and describe what it feels like to be undervalued and discounted simply because of the sex that they are. White men have always had their constitutional rights in full measure. Black citizens fought for the rights that white men have always had receiving the right to vote long ago. Black men have the full rights afforded them in the amendment to the constitution long after the white men who wrote it for themselves did. Females of every color are still fighting for equality, respect and basic human rights afforded all men. "It is impossible to realize our goals while discriminating against half the human race. As study after study has taught us, there is no tool for development more effective than the empowerment of women" Kofi Annan, Then UN Secretary-General, 2006 (Half the Sky Page 185).

There are too many other issues that women face to discuss in full detail in this short amount of time. I will name them so that there may be a conscious awareness that the many issues women face and are challenged by everyday around the globe are many. The first is equal pay for equal work, sexual harassment in the workplace, the glass ceiling which is alive and well. The disparity of time spent doing household chores, caring for everyone else in their families not realizing their own potential, gender stereotypes in the media, being objectified daily, domestic violence and violence of all kinds toward women, educational barriers and the list goes on.

When I look at the sociological perspectives on the subject of gender inequality and what we have learned about the different theories these are my conclusions in summary. "Symbolic Interactionists talk about how society uses labels male and female to sort its members into separate groups, a process that starts within the family and is reinforced by social institutions" (Henslin Page 267). "This socialization process is an effective way we learn to evaluate ourselves on the basis of how well we do gender" (Henslin Page 267). I agree that labels are part of the problem. It is also a self-fulfilling prophecy. When we label anything it slants our perspective and takes away the value of learning who and what someone is individually. Functionalists have their opinion about how the domination of women came to be but in today's world how does inequality and discrimination serve as a function? What function does it serve in today's societies? Unlike other subjects we have discussed and how Functionalists explain the function of a particular social problem this theory in this circumstance leads me to see this theory as obsolete. Sort of like the idea that "this is the way it's always been done so why change it" kind of mentality. There is no value in the function of discrimination unless you are the one who by discrimination keeps his power and control. The word that comes to mind is dysfunction.

The Conflict Feminist perspective says that "Social equality comes about by forcing those in power to yield – for those in power do not willingly cede their control of society's institutions" (Henslin Page 272). This has been the struggle for two to three hundred years for women in this country. Women continue to slowly make gains by forced and legal means for equality. It is my opinion at this juncture that these gains have not been anywhere near fast enough, large enough or real enough. Anytime women gain we also seem to and do step back in other ways. Media, music, lyrics, television shows, and commercials all shout to the world and to every little girl what is expected of them. How they should look, how they should act points down to each generation of young women who are vulnerable to their messages. The images and words are still saying that women are objects of a sexual nature and that this is where their value lies. What can be done to make changes and to continue to make changes?

Humanitarian efforts can have a residual effect for those who help. As humans when working for the greater good and when we give to a greater, larger cause than ourselves it tends to help make us happier and more satisfied humans.

If I were to research this social issue further I would read more women's history books to find out more about the reality of the legacy of women in history. There are many great websites and organizations out there fighting the good fight for social change for women. I would also read more about how one person can make a difference in awareness of the problems women face and the solutions to those problems. The more you know about an issue the more you can do to make others aware. The more people who are aware who take steps to change will someday change the tide to something more real and lasting for women.

Abusive Relationships

Domestic Violence

Laurie A. Ault

Lake Tahoe Community College

Psychology 103 – Adulthood and Aging

Katie Guiney Olsen, Instructor

June 7, 2014

ABUSIVE RELATIONSHIPS – DOMESTIC

VIOLENCE

Abstract

Domestic Abuse is very common in our country and crosses every socioeconomic boundary. This essay includes statistics on the prevalence of domestic abuse whether it is verbal, emotional or physical abuse. Women and men can be victims of this crime and the cost to families and society is enormous. This essay offers some solutions to ending the abusive relationship either by asking for change or ending the abusive relationship. The information contained here includes suggestions for counseling and therapy as well as solutions and help information for women, men and their families. Domestic Violence education is the key as well as anger management and life coping skills in order to help men and women engage in healthier relationships.

ABUSIVE RELATIONSHIPS

I think that what I want to first address in this essay about abusive relationships is this. I think because of the way media and society see women as well as the ways we are taught to think about women and how to treat women it makes it easier for men to justify how they treat women. The first step in abuse is a thought process about the undervaluing of people including the self. The way our society displays and views women, talks about women and in general models behaviors about how women are to be thought about, treated and undervalued is the reason it is not too many steps to verbal abuse which then leads to actual physical abuse.

Simply because of outdated views many times men are not educated about doing life differently women remain in subjugated positions. These are not just my opinions they are based in fact. (Ault, Laurie) "The statistics around domestic violence are staggering: in the United States, one in every four women experience severe physical violence from an intimate partner at some point in their lifetimes. Over 15 million children witness violence in their homes each year. Most incidents are never reported to the police. One in 4 women will experience domestic violence during her lifetime. Women experience more than 4 million physical assaults and rapes because of their partners. Men are victims of nearly 3 million physical assaults. Women are more likely to be killed by an intimate partner than men. Women ages 20 to 24 are at greatest risk of becoming victims of domestic violence. Every year, 1 in 3 women who is a victim of homicide is murdered by her current or former partner (National Center for Victims of Crime) http://www.victimsofcrime.org/media/reporting-on-child-sexual-abuse/child-sexual-abuse-statistics

Though exact legal definitions vary depending on where you are located, domestic violence can generally be defined as a pattern of abusive behavior characterized by the intent to gain or maintain power and control over an intimate partner or other family members. The abuse can be established over time and in most cases, it begins subtly with insults, a shove or by alienating a survivor from family and friends. With time, the abusive behavior can be more frequent and increase in severity. Domestic violence can take many forms, including physical, sexual, emotional, verbal, economic and/or psychological abuse. It affects people of all ages, sexual orientations, religions, genders, socioeconomic backgrounds and education levels, and takes place in all kinds of relationships. Domestic violence is a crime rooted in power and control—it is never "caused" by making someone angry or upset. It is never justifiable or excusable, nor is it ever the fault of a survivor. All people deserve to be in healthy and loving relationships free of violence. http://www.joyfulheartfoundation.org/learn/domestic-violence

Many factors can contribute to domestic violence, but none excuse hurting another person. Partners who are in healthy relationships respond to problems by talking things out together—or sometimes by seeking therapy—and do not turn to controlling or abusive behavior. You have a right to be respected in all aspects of your relationship. The roots of domestic violence and other types of violent relationships are linked to power and control. If one partner feels the need to dominate the other in any shape or form, whether it is physical, sexual, emotional, economic or psychological, then it is significantly more likely a relationship will turn violent. Research has shown that people with abusive tendencies generally turn violent when they feel out of control. It is important to note that abuse is a learned behavior, which, in some cases could have been learned early on in childhood. An abuser may have witnessed domestic violence in his or her home and understood that violence was a means of maintaining control in the family unit.

"If you overlook disrespect and unkind words they will continue to come. In order to change the dynamic, you have to be willing to say "I don't deserve to be spoken to like that." You need to say "Stop it" Do not engage in this type of exchange. If necessary, you must walk away. Do not play with him verbally. What I mean is do not engage in verbal sparring" (Ault, Laurie).

It is a fact that men are also the victims of verbal abuse and are harassed daily by women who suffer from the same sense of loss of control and the need to feel power and control over her sons, her daughters and her husband or partner. This type of female is teaching her sons and daughters to behave in the same way eventually victimizing others in their partnerships and relationships. There are better ways to live. I suggest the following ideas and strategies in order to make positive changes in your life and the lives of your children if you have them.

Trust your feelings about the abuse. Many verbal abusers create self-doubt in the victim, having you question whether or not you are actually being abused. If you are feeling unsafe, sad or hurt by anything your partner is saying to you, and these things happen on a consistent basis, you are being verbally abused. Stand your ground when your partner begins the abusive tirade. Shut him down immediately by either walking away or telling him you will not stand for his insults any longer" (Ault, Laurie).

Try repeating a selected phrase over and over, in a normal tone of voice at a normal volume such as "I am not going to listen to this" or "When you calm down, we can talk."

Ask your partner to stop calling you names or yelling. You may also want to ask him (or her) why he feels the need to call you names or insult you in any way. Speaking in a quiet voice might force your partner to stop yelling in order to hear what you are saying.

Suggest counseling and offer to go with your partner. Some abusers were themselves victims and are reacting to past trauma. Helping your partner deal with his inner demons may eliminate the verbal abuse from your relationship.

End the relationship if the verbal abuse continues and your attempts to counter or end it are unsuccessful. Not every person is willing to change and you deserve to be treated with dignity and respect. Humanitarian efforts can have a residual effect for those who help. As humans when working for the greater good and when we give to a greater, larger cause than ourselves it tends to help make us happier and more satisfied humans.

"No one deserves to be undervalued and treated with disrespect." (Ault, Laurie).

On the following pages I am listing west coast resources that will be helpful. You can Google resource listings for every area in the United States as well as National Resources. I found the website www.feministmajority.org to be a fantastic website to help find any possible resource you could need or use as a referral for anyone you may know who could use direction in asking for help.

This website also works for Political Policy Advocacy to Advance Equality.

Laurie Ault
Josh Fleming, Instructor
English 103
December 11, 2013

The Inequality of Women

The Unspoken Issue – Civil Rights, Equal Rights and
Human Rights

In the eyes of the world women are still seen as less than. Most Americans are willing to not talk about or see the problems that women still face in this country when it comes to inequality in the work force, in the home and in society. It is my contention that this is the last real ALLOWED discrimination not only in this country but in the world. For the sake of illuminating the subject a comparative will be shown between the similarities between sex discrimination and racial discrimination.

Is the inequality of women the same issue as racism is/was? Why does inequality for women remain? Why are women seen as "less" than across the globe? Why was Malala shot in the head by Taliban simply for promoting education for girls and women? Why globally do we not have the same access to education, equal pay for equal work? Why are there millions of girls enslaved globally and used for sex trafficking?

Why are all of these modes of operation allowed to continue across the globe and across time?

Inequalities still remain in the United States of America. Sexual Harassment statistics show that over time there has been little if any improvement even though policies have been put into place in this country to protect women and men from sexual harassment in the work environment. For example, in 1997 30.7% of claims filed and in 2011 there were 28.5% claims filed according to the Knowledge Center and from the Equity in Business Leadership Centers article titled, "Sex Discrimination and Sexual Harassment. "Race discrimination is the only other complaint brought to the EEOC more often at 35.4%". "46% of women believe they've experienced sex discrimination in the workplace according to a survey from 2013." One of the other items of concern, especially for women in the workplace is pay disparities that continue. Even though women are increasingly becoming the ones who hold degrees and who also have equal or better qualifications than men in the same situation it is more and more clear that the differences in pay have to do with sex discrimination.

> "Pay disparities over a lifetime can be as much as $700,000.00 if the woman is a high school graduate, 1.2 million if she is a college graduate, and 2 million if she is a professional school graduate. This information is from calculating, "Over the

course of a woman's life based on 47 years working full time year round". (Dept. Of Economic and Social Affairs – The World's Women 2010, Trends and Statistics Report)

When women come home from work there is a fairly good chance that there is a power struggle going on here as well. There are struggles about the division of labor in the home even though women work outside the home like their male counterparts, the women's work is never done. These days it is called the second shift for women. According to Colette McIntyre in her article "Despite More Female Breadwinners "Second Shift Is Still a Thing," "on an average day 82% of women and 65% of men spent some time doing household activities such as housework, cooking, lawn care or financial and other household management." "On an average day, 20% of men did housework such as cleaning or doing laundry compared with 48% of women. Thirty-nine percent of men did food preparation or clean up compared with 65% of women" (McIntyre).

Many women were taught from the moment they were born that their role is to do the housework, make dinners, nurture the family and much more. As society has changed more and more women have entered the work force adding to the work load of women. The gender role that women are taught and have bought into over time is somewhat outdated as they have not demanded a more equitable division of labor in the home. The debate over how we learn our role in society has existed for decades. Is it nature and nurture or evolution, genetics and biology that shape our gender identities? Margaret Mead conducted a study when travelling to New Guinea in the 1930's where she lived with three different tribes. Mead concluded after living with these three tribes that "masculine and feminine are culturally taught rather than biologically determined" (Lindsey, Page 25, 26). In really explaining the differences between men and women there is really too much focus on the biological differences and not enough on the "institutional androcentrism" that transforms male-female differences into female disadvantage" (Lindsey Page 51-52). There are many who argue these days for biological factors largely shaping gender identity. I don't agree with those who would argue this point. I believe our pop culture and the media have quite a bit to do with how people in the United States view gender roles. Many of today's young girls and women are being brainwashed by media in most forms.

The media takes the sex difference theme and exploits' it. Soon people believe that "men have math and promiscuity genes and women have caring and victimization genes that predestine their gender roles" (Lindsey Page 52). "Pop-Darwinism becomes a convenient moral guide to justify assertions about male sexuality and female passivity" (McCaughey, 2008) (Lindsey Page 52).

Family and environment only play a part in our ideas about gender roles. "Beginning at about age three television becomes another potent socializer" "in all age and racial categories, heavy television viewing is strongly associated with adherence to traditional and stereotyped views about gender" (Lindsey Page 360). The media advertising still shown in magazines today are not far from the ever present traditional roles ascribed to women. Surely you must have noticed that women in television commercial ads are the ones using the mop, cleaning the bathroom, and buying the vacuum. Magazine articles talk about some health information for women, but the larger majority of articles are about how to keep a man happy sexually, and advice about beauty and relationships.

It appears that after the women's movement in the 1970's it did not take long for things to return to the more traditional roles a decade after the movement. The sex sells mentality is still the norm and it appears to be worse than ever. Women are shown scantily clad while men's faces are shown in ads. "Such depictions are reinforced by how much of the body is shown in an ad. Males represent "face-isms," in that their faces are photographed more often than their bodies. Females represent "body-isms" or partial-isms" in that their bodies or parts of their bodies are more often shown" (Lindsey Page 363). How will we ever change the gender stereotypes that are old and worn out? Ads with young girls in bras and underwear are shown during the family hour of television every night over and over. These ladies look as if they are about fifteen. Yet, this has become the norm. These images only used to be viewed in the likes of Playboy magazine but are now everywhere you look. Thus underscoring the idea that the top value of a woman lies in the way she looks and her sexuality. What are some of ways we can begin to change these old fashioned ideas?

Socialization is key to making many of the changes in equity between the sexes for the future. Is this an impossible dream? Sociobiologists' argue that evolutionary theory can be used to draw conclusions about humans from studies of animals." "Like other animals, humans, are structured by nature (biology) with an innate drive to ensure that their individual genes are passed on to the next generation" (Lindsey Page 25, 26)." "Gender roles are connected with different sexual scripts – one considered more appropriate for males, and the other considered more appropriate for females." Culture and socialization affect our ideas of what our roles should be. "Parent child interactions occur in a cultural context in which females have lower power and prestige than males." "Beginning in infancy, parents socialize their sons to express emotions differently than daughters in ways that support gender differences in power"' (Lindsey Page 55).

There are so many factors that have an effect on how we learn our roles in society. Media sends messages about how women and girls are to behave bombarding us every day. Men have the same types of images coming at them but not in such a large and massive way. Women are told and sold that it is not ok to get old, have wrinkles, be well nourished, not be sexy, you name it. The media in commercials show women in their gender associated roles and continue to sell the ideas of what it is to be feminine. Women seem to fall for this message and so do men. Women allow themselves to be trapped in a subordinate position in order to be liked and to get along. The roles that women are trained for seem to make it easier for them to be victims. For example, when it comes to rape and other types of harassment or assault the statistics are huge.

One of the facts that are astounding in the United States of America is that over 22 million women have been raped in their lifetime. (National Intimate Partner and Sexual Violence Survey 2010) One out of five American women has been the victim of an attempted or completed rape in their lifetime. One million two hundred and seventy thousand women are raped each year. Another six million six hundred and forty-six thousand are victims of other sexual crime, including sexual coercion, unwanted sexual contact, or unwanted sexual experiences. (Department of Justice 2010). The statistics of crimes against women in this country are staggering. It would seem that since these issues are difficult in some cases for women to talk about the crimes or incidences could be underreported making the numbers higher.

The United Nations defines violence against women as "any act of gender based violence that results in, or is likely to result in physical, sexual or mental harm or suffering to women, including threats of such acts, coercion or arbitrary deprivation of liberty, whether occurring in public or in private life." (http://www.who.int/mediacentre/factsheets/fs239/en/index.html)

Worldwide violence against women is an epidemic. This has major repercussions resulting in health problems for women and their children. Violence against women is a violation of the woman's human rights. In China and other countries, it is common practice to decide not to take female children to the doctor or hospital when they are ill "resulting in 39,000 baby girls dying annually because parents don't give them the same medical care and attention the boys receive" (Half The Sky, Introduction, xiv). In South Asia and the Muslim world similar patterns emerge. "In India a "bride burning" – to punish a woman for an inadequate dowry or to eliminate her so a man can remarry – takes place approximately once every two hours" (Half The Sky, Introduction, xiv).

> One hundred seven million females are missing from the globe today. Every year at least another two million girls worldwide

disappear because of gender discrimination. The worst of these abuses tend to occur in poor nations, but the United States and other Western Nations are not immune" (Half The Sky, Introduction xv).

Statistics are usually not so interesting, but there are more to follow. Armed with information we can all make the steps individually that will change the world. THIS IS IMPORTANT AND ASTOUNDING

"The global statistics on the abuse of girls are numbing. It appears that more girls have been killed in the last fifty years, precisely because they were girls, than men were killed in all the battles of the twentieth century. More girls are killed in this routine "gendercide" in any one decade than people were slaughtered in all the genocides of the twentieth century" (Half the Sky, Introduction, Page xvii).

The other injustices women face has to do with their access to equal education or education in general. In many places across the globe it is seen as unnecessary to educate girls and women.

Educational challenges for women worldwide keep women from being able to break the cycle and stand on their own two feet. Many times and in many countries women are treated as property and they have no rights. They are forced to marry at young ages and are often beaten, raped and thrown away if they cause any trouble. Many are murdered by their partners. Women are not valued in many countries so men are extremely violent against them treating them as property. There are people everywhere who are working hard to make a difference in the lives of women and girls and in so doing is also having an effect on helping young boys to receive more opportunities in education as well. Slowly things have improved in some nations and in some ways.

Progress has been made in educating boys and girls in primary education according to the United Nations Report. "Measurable progress has been made towards greater gender parity in primary enrollment, with gender gaps diminishing in most regions of the world. Positive global trends in primary enrollment, however, obscure uneven progress and some slippage or stagnation. While the overall progress in primary education in the past decade is encouraging, major barriers stand in the way of progress: 72 million children – 54 per cent of them girls – are out of school." (UN Report Page 8) "Long hours of work affect children's ability to participate fully in education. Analysis shows that school attendance declines as the number of hours spent on household chores increases – and declines more steeply for girls than for boys." (UN Report Page 10)

"The impact of educating girls is much greater than the individual. It enables women to have a greater impact on reducing poverty in their communities, as

within most communities, women are responsible for providing food, health care and education of their families."
(http://www.globalpovertyproject.com/infobank/wome n).

"We live in a world in which women living in poverty face gross inequalities and injustice from birth to death. From poor education to poor nutrition to vulnerable and low pay employment, the sequence of discrimination that a woman may suffer during her entire life is unacceptable but all too common." (http://www.globalpovertyproject.com/infobank/wome n)

The wide spread discrimination of women globally in every area of their lives is a challenge and sometimes a fight for survival. Historically, this is a struggle that we are aware of, but it seems we do not speak about too much in this country, The United States of America. Recently, I had an instructor tell me, "Well it's a lot better here in America than everywhere else." This was a male instructor. He is right, it is better here in some ways than everywhere else. Women have more rights and are afforded more educational opportunities than many other countries. But, because it is better here in some ways, does that excuse and make it ok that women still face discrimination much like that of the slaves of the 19th century?

Until very recently in time, women did not have the right to vote, own property, be afforded credit, inherit property and the list goes on. These rights were not afforded to women even after the slaves were freed and the black man was given the right to vote when the fifteenth amendment to the constitution was ratified in 1870. (The United States Constitution) Women have only had the right to vote in this country for LESS than the last 100 years. The struggles to gain freedoms and rights in our own country have been slow and inequitable. If we look at the treatment of black people in our not too distant past, we can see some very stark similarities in how women are still treated today.

Booker T. Wright was a black man in 1960's Mississippi. He talked about the menu, talked about how the men there called him boy or Booker or nigger. He spoke with a sort of lyrical, tone using the one he used to stay out of trouble with the white men. He had to put up with cow towing to all of the superior attitudes of the white men while he served them every day. At the end of the day Booker would go work in his own diner serving the black population there. By the end of Booker's introduction to his working conditions and the menu he served, his entire demeanor changes as he begins to talk about how he wants things to be different for his children. He wants for them an education and the ability to live in harmony with everyone. He does not want them to have to go to work in an all-white diner and demean themselves, saying yes sir and no sir to white men and people who would treat him as less than just because of the color of their skin. "Booker Wright, who worked at a local "whites only" restaurant, allowed himself to be filmed for a documentary. In this short clip of "Booker he delivers a heartfelt monologue about his true feelings about serving the white community, and about his aspirations for his children, who he hoped would grow up free from the prejudice he faced". (The Grio.com)

I watched this segment about Booker on Dateline and I could identify completely with this man of color and his pain at being discriminated against simply because of the color of his skin. This is something I understand. I am not an ethnic human being. I am not gay and I am not handicapped, but I am a woman. Who hasn't heard women referred to as bitches, dumb blondes, airheads, and the weaker sex? From the first moments I can remember it was an unspoken message by actions of others around me that boys were more valued and not only had more to offer the world but that they also had more opportunities and more doors would open to them simply because they have a penis. There is no measuring of the intelligence of men, it is simply because they have different body parts they are automatically seen as being able to do more and be more.

How would you feel if you were told from the moment you were old enough to understand that you are less important, less smart, less strong and that you could never hope to be anything of value, never be allowed to be educated or put your talents to use? Never mind being afforded the luxury of finding out what your talents are simply because you have different body parts? Would you be offended if you were told in a myriad of ways that your major or only value as a human being was that you were an object, a sexual object and that is all? All across the globe women are seen as non-essential and to be used by men for whatever purpose they decide. They are used as a means to an end and are not respected as the individuals that they are. Men think nothing of killing the women they cannot control or they are afraid they cannot control.

It is no longer politically correct to publicly demean and call names about Jewish people, Mexican people, black people, handicapped people or any ethnic group, but it is still ok to demean women, to discount and diminish them through the media, at home, at school and in the workplace. Why is discrimination against women allowed to go on? Why has society not stepped up like they did for civil rights in the 1960's and also when outlawing slavery?

The information given in this essay of course has a point. The things you can do for positive change are many. I will conclude with ideas and also concrete ways in which you and others can help enlighten others and enlist their help in this global fight for the equality of women. Simple things each individual can do is writing letters, sending money or volunteering your time.

Go to www.globalgiving.org or www.kiva.org and open an account. Global giving lets you choose a grass roots project to which to give money in education health, disaster relief, or more than a dozen other areas around the developing world. Sponsor a girl through Plan International, Women for Women International, World Vision, or American Jewish World Service. Sign up for updates on www.womensenews.org or www.worldpulse.com. Join the CARE Action Network at www.can.care.org. This will help you speak out. This is a citizen's advocacy group. (Half The Sky, Page 252)

Information and actions you can take are on these sites.

Humanitarian efforts can have a residual effect for those who help. As humans when working for the greater good and when we give to a greater, larger cause than ourselves it tends to help make us happier and more satisfied humans.

END OF THIS ESSAY
All of the works cited/sources for these essays are listed in the bibliography at the end of this book.

Comments from the instructor

"What I liked most about your essay was that it made me think and make connections. Your essay peels away the layers of familiarity and tolerance we have for gender discrimination, offering a historical and present perspective rife with statistics and anecdotes. I appreciate the solutions you put forth as well as the personal investment you have in this essay. I am so pleased you were a part of my class." – Josh

Now that I have repeated all of the components that are involved in a power over relationship I strongly hope that what I have intended in writing this book will be contemplated. Some who read this will not have encountered this information before. It was and is my hope that this printed information will be of help to you in your journey.

As you can tell from reading each chapter, I feel very strongly about women's issues as they are human issues. There are many inequities across the globe that need to be attended to as quickly as possible. Discrimination of ANY kind should not be tolerated in this globally connected world. The way we educate our citizens needs to be changed. We somehow try to overlook bullying and the social hierarchy that exists.

If we all treated each other with kindness, if we taught this behavior in schools as being one of the most important things to be learned as humans, if we taught real tolerance of differences, if we are taught not to be afraid of differences we could slowly change the world.

It seems that many of these issues while being discussed get a lot of lip service. The old poem that hung in my room as a child said: Children Learn What They Live.

It is that simple.

Children Learn What Live

If a Child lives with CRITICISM,
   He learns to CONDEM.
If a child lives with HOSTILITY,
   He learns to FIGHT.
If a child lives with RIDICULE,
   He learns to be SHY.
If a child lives with SHAME,
   He learns to feel GUILTY.
If a child lives with TOLERANCE,
   He learns to be PATIENT.
If a child lives with ENCOURAGEMENT,
   He learns CONFIDENCE.
If a child lives with PRAISE,
   He learns to APPRECIATE.
If a child lives with FAIRNESS,
   He learns JUSTICE.
If a child lives with SECURITY,
   He learns to have FAITH.
If a child lives with APPROVAL,
   He learns to LIKE HIMSELF.
If a child lives with ACCEPTANCE and FRIENDSHIP,
   He learns to find LOVE IN THE WORLD.

Author, Dorothy Law Nolte
(Of course we as women must fill in and change the
word to she where he has been written)

Is there anybody out there?

Means to an end

And lastly I find I must address this type of issue in the difference between men and women. Warning here: I am speaking very candidly. It is not my intent to offend it is my intent to just say this as it seems. I cannot imagine I am alone in this scenario.

Are we really just a means to an end? This question comes to mind because of recent discussions with a longtime friend. The subject matter caused me to contemplate this issue between some men and women. Sooner or later does everyone out there show their true colors? Does everyone have a secret side to themselves that is kept hidden but that sooner or later must show itself and come into the light for inspection? Because I am a woman my experience with men has been, well interesting is the nicest and less difficult word to use. Do all men have secrets and do all men hide under the mask of "Nice Guy?" I cannot tell you how many times I have met and started to get to know a man based on what he shows me as who he is, and sooner or later the mask begins to slip just enough for me to wonder – uh oh – is this a glimpse of the real guy and his motivations under the surface?

I think the reason I ask the questions is because women generally operate with different motivations in relationships with men. This is the reason women can get hurt with more frequency. So I ask are women really just a means to a man's end so to speak? I have the tendency to think so. At least for many.

I suppose if men were more up front about it then who would care? Probably the only thing that might change is that men might not get laid as frequently but maybe then they could actually really believe they are a good guy.   What I am saying is – this disguise is about the scenario when a man tells you he is attracted to you and wants to see you. This may be true... or not... What he may really be saying is I want to get laid. We are attracted to one another so let's get together. What he may really be saying, (or doing) is throwing out bait to see what you will do with it. Maybe he wants a variety of different women to sleep with to feed his ego. Different women to warm his bed for each night of the week or weekend.

How many men have you heard say they have a "f" buddy? This means he is getting laid regularly already by some lady who he will never take seriously or be a contender for his affection. The actual physical act is what is most important, but he is free to cast his net out there frequently to see who will come over and having done this behavior frequently enough he tells himself he is just enjoying the benefits of being "single." Operating under false pretenses by saying he is interested in following up on the vibe or the attraction this experience can often lead to a one-night stand or if he likes you enough you may even be able to replace the current "f buddy." All of the benefits without the attachments.

I think this is a way many single men operate and do enjoy being **single because they use the idea or the hope of an attachment with a woman as bait to engage her.** I think that this is one of the nastiest things a man can do with a woman who can have the best of intentions, and who is herself real and authentic. Men can use a woman's own belief system about how relationships go (you like me, I like you, we get together to get to know each other better) and see what happens next. The hope of a possible real relationship is used against her because she is being real and he is only after the excitement of the conquest or conquering and even thinks to himself – how long it might take and how much wine will have been drunk before both parties are naked and engaged in sex. First the bait is thrown out there, the woman responds and the bet is made mentally by the man about how long it will take to achieve the objective. The problem with this scenario is that the woman typically has no idea that she has just participated in the catch and release program that this type of guy is involved in. Obviously a woman can say no somewhere in the mix, but if a man is really good at this type of attraction and if he plays his cards right he can repeat this behavior until the cows come home thinking he has done absolutely nothing wrong.

Of course there are women who don't mind a one-night stand; they want to get laid also. It was fun and so on but I would wager a bet of my own. I would wager that more often than not women who are hopeful and open to a date or who have known this type of man as a friend who feel safe and as though he cares about her feelings and who may appear as a gentleman is not what he seems. The only thing that is different from a guy who is young and who does this behavior and a man who is older is the sophistication of the disguise. I do realize that dating today has become more like speed dating. People do seem to cut to the chase faster and women certainly can do this to a guy who is authentically looking for a relationship. They don't want to waste their time and think they can figure out a person in a twenty-minute conversation at Starbucks. If you have met on a dating site, then meet in person men are many times trying to find out if you are pretty enough or not. Or smart enough, or tall enough or whatever is most important to them at any given moment. I find it all rather depressing in some ways and I suppose I could actually get very irritated about the way people treat each other these days, but it would do no good. I am sure this type of activity has to be very hard on people who are shy or slow to warm up. Those who find it hard to open up to others or who are slower to trust must have one heck of a time.

So, being female I must address this issue from a perspective of my experience. I have found over time that many men view women as a means to an end in that they are using us to satisfy whatever they may find is missing from their world.

A sex object is or can be at the top of the list. What is required is that you have the right parts. Most guys when you say – sure come on over and if you want to talk and get to know each other better will most likely not show up. They don't want to talk much – they want to cut to the chase and get laid in the least painful most direct way. Charm, a little conversation and most likely a few drinks. I am not saying anything that most people don't already know but I do have to say that recent experience with men I have known and trusted over time have also let me down because the mask slipped just enough with them to show me that ultimately what was most important to them was their own agenda, their own motivations and they could have cared less about the damage it caused in our relationships which I had thought to be based in respect and the shared value of each other and each relationship.

What it boiled down to though in the end was that many times we can be a means to their end on any given day. Ultimately these men who are in their late 50's and early 60's were playing the same games as men I had known when I was in my late teens and early twenty's. It was all about their ego, making a woman find them desirable and playing into the attention given to get in a woman's pants. I know this entire dissertation must sound like – dah – really?

What I am trying to say is that after the dust settles and the bait is set, it can be easy to fall for this. Because this has happened to many of us the fallout after can be feeling naive, and not valued as a human person. I know when it (IT) had happened to me in my lifetime and as a younger person I could not see this treatment coming. I felt almost violated mentally and emotionally because my reality was so different from the men I thought I knew.

I come at relationships honest, open and authentically myself. They gave the appearance of that, but under the mask was the real motivation which was to catch and release. The only thing that changes is how long they keep you before they release you. If they are experts at this – you will still always think they are a good guy, they will think they are a good guy, and their behavior will continue leaving some destruction along the way. Mostly, these men won't even notice you are missing from their lives when the dust settles because they do not care about the carnage left. They do not see it nor do they feel it. These men are Narcissistic men who are limited in the depth of the feelings they have about anything. It is all about them and there is no real empathy. Everything is an illusion including the story they tell you about who they really are.

Three Things

Cannot Long

Stay Hidden

The Sun, The Moon

And The Truth -

Buddha

Chapter 15

After Forward

For an abused woman, leaving the relationship is never a single act.

It is always a process.

The process of escaping from domestic abuse is one of quiet strengthening.

It can happen so silently, over such a long period of time,

that you will be unaware of it.

You may even feel frustrated, because your words and actions

Seem to be having no impact.

It seems as though nothing is happening.

She looks as though she is a passive participant in her life,

willing to swallow whatever her abuser dishes out.

But don't be too sure of that.

There is a parallel in the insect world.

Substantial energy is required for a moth to lift itself in flight.

The wing muscles must reach a certain critical temperature

Before they can move the wings fast enough to let the moth fly.

Until that temperature is reached, flight is impossible.

Chapter 16
Unspoken Sins

One of the biggest heartbreaks in my lifetime is the realization that women are still not seen as equal human beings. The codes of conduct, the rules for women in our society, in this country still promote the inequality of women. I commented one day in class to my Sociology Professor exactly that. I also said I had hoped we (women) would have come much farther since the late 60's early 1970's when we had momentum in the women's movement. His response was immediate surprise and then he said "Really?" He at the time was in his 40's and was married happily with no children. He taught about the woman as a "Spectacle." He taught about gender issues from a Sociological standpoint, yet he was surprised by my passionate comments. But, of course he could only really have one perspective, and even though he knew about inequality in a practical sense he had never heard a woman, and certainly not a woman my age say such a thing. He was surprised that this subject and this issue was at the very top of my lifetime regrets list. I only have a couple of regrets.

One of the other is what I have said previously. I regret losing more than ten years in a negative marriage relationship. All told I had lost close to 20. I still want to find the 10 or so years I lost and plan to live until the age of 105 to make up for it. LOL.

When I was a young teenager, I was whistled at, jeered at, stared at, talked to in such a way as to be unnerved and scared. I was yelled at frequently as I walked anywhere. I was approached by people in cars; I was harassed at 16 while driving down a freeway. Scared out of my wits because a bunch of guys in a car decided it would be fun to drive fast behind me and then next to me on a stretch of highway where there was little traffic, but they blocked my exit and my escape. When I was 14 I was chased down my own street, one man jumping out of a truck chasing me while the other waited in the vehicle. I ran to a friend's house escaping just barely. I have never been as afraid before or since. To this day I wonder if he had caught me if I would still be here to tell about it. It was the 70's and I did not tell anyone. The police were never called. It was a deep dark secret, as though I had done something wrong. After that, I was afraid to babysit, afraid of dark streets. I was afraid to be alone in my house at night.

When I was 16 I had friends over for a get together and dance. I had a steady boyfriend at the time. Some drank beer and one was my boyfriend. He drank too much and fell asleep.

One of the boys at the party decided this was a great opportunity to sexually assault me. He said what are you going to do scream? I knew if I screamed, things would turn very ugly. I had said no and it did not matter. Again, this was still the 70's. When I was twenty, I went to my regular gynecologists' appointment and while examining me my Doctor sexually assaulted me. Again I did not report it, did not call the police because that would have caused untold problems. The shame involved should not have been mine. I told him, "Doctor just do your job." I did not go back there. I do regret not reporting this for the sake of others. I had no support from anywhere. I felt ashamed and embarrassed. So, I stuffed this in my bad experiences box and felt shame for many years. I would have reported it as I grew and gained confidence, but the Doctor died from a heart attack. There were never any consequences for him as he had probably assaulted many along the way. Many women do not report these acts by men in positions of power. Apparently no one ever reported him as he continued to practice medicine and deliver babies until he died.

I was sexually harassed by my boss to the point where I felt like I would lose my job. I have been sexually assaulted when asleep. The thing is, my stories are crimes or offenses that were committed against me, but as I tell this it seems like somehow I would be, could be blamed for what happened. I did not ask for these things to happen to me, they just did. I was always careful, I never showed off my body, I never flirted, I almost actually hid to the point of making myself as invisible as I could possibly be. I did not dress in such a way to ask for it, I wanted no part of this. I remember having a red dress when I was twenty that I was afraid to wear because it seemed too risky. I knew if I wore anything that was form fitting it would attract unwanted attention. I tried to be careful. I did not show cleavage on purpose. Why did it happen? Because I am female.   I am also a person, a human being. It seems as though that should be a simple concept and be the one that is considered by others first and foremost.

Along the way at various ages I had boyfriends slap me across the face, choke me, belittle me, and make thousands of comments that had accumulated over the years.   The comments came from everywhere. Husbands, boyfriends, strangers, neighbors' other guys from school, at work, you name it. Society's men had no boundaries. At least many did not. My next door neighbor once made lewd comments to me and he and his father would peer at me through the fence or try to see in my bedroom window. I never told a soul.

Does this type of thing still go on? After all, it is way past the women's movement and women's liberation where we demanded our rights. We are not supposed to be harassed at work, at school, and other places. But does it still go on? Are we still sucking it up and letting it go? Are we still being silent to a larger degree? Yes, we had been silent.

I wrote the above questions in 2013-2015 because I knew the status quo was alive and well. And then came the election in 2016. The match has been lit and the fire is now burning.

What follows are my comments about the dangers of so many accusations against men in the media. I understand the need to get the complaints by women out against whomever made unwanted moves, comments and just plain acted inappropriately. This was and could still be far too common. I certainly understand the sexual assault charges filed against those who went so far as to touch or assault women when they have said no very clearly and those who abused their positions of power, sometimes paying off women to keep silent. If a man has assaulted or raped a woman this must be reported.   I understand why these crimes have finally been stated out loud.

I do have some concerns about some who have decided to talk about things that made them uncomfortable, or comments that were made that may have been inappropriate, but these comments are far different than assault.

It is my feeling we need to be discerning about how we ask for change now.

The danger in the current climate we face as we march, and as we tell the world and add our voices to the me too movement, as we pile on all of the various voices about our experiences in the world as objects we must fine tune what it is that we truly want the world to know. We do not want the message to be lost in the uproar.

The reports in the news every day for several months now have been one more and then one more famous person (celebrity) telling about how a rich, powerful man had made advances that were unwanted or did not take no for an answer as he played grab what he could while we hurriedly walked out a door. These accusations are mixed in with actual sexual assault and rape. They are mixed in with comments about how some were being verbally made to feel uncomfortable.

There is a spectrum of things that can be said and done that are minor misunderstandings that happen between men and women, but are not crimes (this also happens when women in this day and age also do this to men) Misunderstandings happen, signals are misread. We cannot be up in arms over this perceived mistreatment by either sex. If the world perceives that we are complaining about every minor detail instead of hears what we are really saying, then we will have won nothing in the search for change.

Our message could be convoluted or lost. We must make the most of this current opportunity to be clear and to clearly state what exactly it is that we WANT.

The whole point of talking about this issue is to ask for lasting and real change. What is it we are saying? What is it we want? What are the solutions to enact real and lasting change? How do we get what we want? We really need to be clear.

The danger of just throwing out endless accusations that encompass what has occurred from A to Z is this could go on indefinitely because of how "WE" have been collectively treated for the last 50 years and before.

The men involved in our lifetimes were brought up when the messages after World War II were that women still belonged at home in the kitchen, and we were a complement to a man rather than a free thinking independent human who chose to be wherever she ended up. It should not be mandated by a society what our choices are, what we can be, what we can do, what we can wear, whether or not we can be educated, or play sports or get paid the same wage as our male counterpart for the exact same job. Yes, that list is much longer than I just stated, but again the message needs to be clear.

Yes, we are fed up with the conspiracy of silence, the enabling behaviors we tried to ignore over time. The treatment of many women over time by men who have had power and control that we were quietly asked to ignore or not pay attention to, to suck up became enough at last. I do not believe I know anyone personally who has not had some of these behaviors exhibited over time by men they have encountered or has not been assaulted in some way in their lifetimes. If you as a female managed to escape this, then you are one of the lucky few. Our society was set up this way. It is no wonder that these behaviors happened and still were happening. Women have been in the workplace since prior to World War II and these behaviors can be and many times are ingrained as men have seen their behavior as harmless. They may even see these behaviors not only as normal, but may think this is some sort of rite of passage. Again, they have never considered women as individual humans, people with rights and feelings and when the women have said they do not like being treated in this way were discounted, ignored, brushed off as not being serious, they did not really mean it, and so the men soldiered on without consequence. Now we are seeing real consequences for the rich and famous and some others where they are losing their livelihood, are withdrawing in shame, or refuse to admit what they have done. They think if they deny what women are saying it is the best way to proceed hopefully unscathed.

The Flip Side

How some men are hearing what we are saying – the lens from some other perspectives. I use an article just pulled from the internet in February 2018. A gentleman named Michael Haneke weighed in on the #Me-too movement. The title of the article says: "The Witch Hunt Should Be Left in The Middle Ages"

Quoted statements from the article are as follows:

"Michael Haneke has become the latest prominent European artist to lament what he calls a "witch hunt" in the wake of the #Metoo movement. Speaking with Kurier, the Austrian filmmaker said there is no question that "any form of rape or coercion is punishable...But this hysterical pre-judgment which is spreading now, I find absolutely disgusting. And I don't know how many of these accusations related to incidents 20 or 30 years ago are primarily statement that have little to do with sexual assault."

"He qualified his statements saying the current debate is disturbing because of the "blind rage that's not based on facts and the prejudices that destroy the lives of people whose crime has not been proved in numerous cases. People are simply assassinated in the media, ruining lives and careers."

"Asked if this escalation can help transform society for the better, Haneke responded, "Any shi* storm that even comes out on the forums of serious online news outlets after such 'revelations' poisons the social climate. "This makes every argument on this very important subject even more difficult.

This new puritanism imbued with a hatred of men that comes in the wake of the #Metoo movement worries me."

"Suspected actors are cut out of movies and TV series in order not to lose (audiences) Where are we living? In the new middle Ages?"

There are others weighing in. Catherine Deneuve was among 100 women who signed an open letter, slamming what they termed "expeditious justice" spurred by the movement." Article by Peter White from Deadline.

I have used this article under the Fair Use Act in order to educate the public on this issue.

There is much on the internet and elsewhere written on this subject currently. I agree in that Sexual Assault and rapes should be prosecuted and justice should take place. We are still in a society where we are to be innocent until proven guilty and not the other way around. This is the danger in all of the varied accusations floating around out there currently. It is time to talk about solutions now. The solutions discussions should have started long ago when the public became aware of the accusations against Bill Cosby. Even before that we had the issue of Anita Hill and Clarence Thomas and unfortunately many, many more public incidences.

Let us move on to the solutions discussions. The criminal justice system should take care of the more serious of these charges against the men involved when it comes to assault or rape. And, these men truly are innocent until proven guilty. Let us not drown out what it is that we are asking for. What is it we want besides justice? We need to be specific and clear.

I heard a short discussion with Jodie Foster on this subject recently who said besides deep discussion involving how it has been for both sides, and the search for understanding she said "It would be great if it just stopped." She was referring to all of the stuff women have had to put up with from the beginning of time. "We as women would just like for "IT" to stop." Amen.

I think that "IT" may be need to be defined for men to make sure they understand what "IT" is so there are no further misunderstandings.

In 1970 Kate Millett wrote Sexual Politics. A feminist writer of the times said this about Millet, "Betty Friedan had written about the problem that had no name, Kate Millet named it, illustrated it, exposed it, analyzed it."

Sexual Politics was published at the time of an emerging women's liberation movement, and an emerging politics that began to define male dominance as a political and institutional form of oppression.

Kate Millett's Sexual Politics was/is an analysis of patriarchal power. Millet developed the notion that men have institutionalized power over women, and that this power is socially constructed as opposed to biological or innate.

Millet said this, "Sex is deep at the heart of our troubles, unless we eliminate the most pernicious of our systems of oppression, unless we go to the very center of the sexual politic and its sick delirium of power and violence, all our efforts at liberation will only land us again in the same primordial stews."

So now here we are 48 years later. Hmmmm.

I expand on my thoughts about this in the next chapter.

Chapter 17

How we got here

In order to put where we currently are in perspective I have to include and discuss some information about our past history. Just as our history currently is affected by what has come before, in our lens on racial discrimination, groups like Black Americans or Mexican Americans, or Chinese Americans, or Japanese Americans, over time, and then there are Gay Americans and then of course Female Americans, need I go on? Our past history and the stories we have told ourselves have gotten us where we are today when it comes to inclusion or exclusion of groups of people, our perceptions and fears, and in some/many instances our reluctance to change.

Open mindedness when it comes to old bias, old stereotypes, and old scripts that had long defined our culture and our stories still many times lie at the bottom of the shelves of our minds. It is not just white Americans who have shelves with dusty stereotypes. Although many of us would not describe ourselves as bigots or racists many times when we dig down deep we may find we have been taught in our long ago pasts by others, family, media, and history itself to color how we see the world currently.

This brings me to how many men still prescribe to old fashioned ideas about what their role in society is and what it is supposed to be moving forward.

I am seeking understanding here for all. For women who are young or who have not studied women's history I will try to shed some light on just a tiny fragment so that we may see how we got here today.

As I have said in previous chapters to begin, women lacked the vote and therefore political power, they were denied many opportunities open to men. In 1872, Myra Bradwell challenged Illinois law which restricted membership in the state bar to men. The Supreme Court upheld the law. Justice Bradley said in his concurring opinion: "It is true that many women are unmarried and not affected by any of the duties, complications, and incapacities arising out of the married state, but these are exceptions to the general rule. The paramount destiny and mission of woman are to fulfill the noble and benign offices of wife and mother. This is the law of the Creator. And the rules of civil society must be adapted to the general constitution of things, and cannot be based upon exceptional cases."

This particular case as stated occurred in 1872. Think about the fact that this was 146 years ago. Again, also think about the fact that women would not be afforded the RIGHT to vote as a citizen of the land until 50 years after black men. It was 1921 when women officially throughout the United States of America gained the right to vote as equal citizens. This was a mere 97 years ago.

In the history of time men have had their rights always. Women have not until very recently.

In 1928 a man named Dr. David Keller wrote a book called the Sexual Education of the Young Woman. I use this as an example as a very standard way that men saw women and who were taught to see women in very specific roles in society. The views for women were narrow and narrow minded. This way of thinking (this narrowness) came from what they knew at the time and had always known.

In this book the man who wrote it had these credentials. "Dr. Kelly was a fellow of the American Psychiatric Association as well as the Assistant Superintendent at the Western State Hospital in Bolivar, Tennessee. The named book was a part of a Sexual Education Series and Dr. Keller wrote another separate volume about the education of the Young Man."

In the volume which was only 152 pages the published contents were as follows: Chapter 1 Introduction: The Mother and Daughter, Chapter 2 A History of the Young Girl, Chapter 3 The Girl's Obligation to Society, Chapter 4 The Anatomy of the Young Girl, Chapter 5 The Physiology of the Young

Girl, Chapter 6 The Psychology of the Young Girl, Chapter 7

The Hygiene of the Young Girl, Chapter 8, The Question of Prostitution, Chapter 9 The Cost of Immorality, Chapter 10 The Bachelor Girl, Chapter 11 The Working Girl, Chapter 12 What a Young Girl Should Know About Men. Chapter 13 The Girl Beautiful. I suppose I could give a short synapsis on what each chapter holds, but just the titles tell us much of the way society saw a females' role. I personally find it shocking that the general term "girl" was used and not woman, young woman or lady. As a society we still to this day use the word girl to describe grown women. We do not call young men boys long after they are adults. The words used are just one small issue to being seen as less than. Just the word girl does not allow for females to ever fully reach adulthood in the conversation that is had by society even today.

Look at the current shows on television and how even though there is a current women's movement the old outdated ways of speaking about women have yet to change. Let's try looking at the dialog again on television next season where the writers will have had the opportunity to take note and make changes.

Historically the way our societies were set up, the Hierarchy of the Patriarchy automatically put and still puts women and girls on the bottom in every area of living, and of life. It was designed that way from the beginning of time in our culture. The assumption was/is that if a man is physically stronger he is to be the one in charge of all things and all people. Of course we know this is not true in other cultures throughout time, but in the United States of America it has been and is true. It is still true today.

If one watches the people in Hollywood who are filled with the hope that comes when one has said what is true for their experience and the fact that they do include the rest of the world (the rest of us) who have borne these experiences over time along with them, it seems as though they feel better and think things will be changing at last. They know that much work needs to be done.

The trouble is and my concern is that the momentum will fade, the conversations will be shorter, quieter and then slowly we could be lulled into complacency as we had been before. Things have changed from the 70's when it comes to inclusion and laws that have changed. One of the major things that did not change although everyone was forced into watching videos on sexual harassment in the work place is that the dialog on (once again) television and out in the world, on social media platforms and even when we speak to friends in our own neighborhoods has remained much the same as before. Song lyrics (rap, hip hop) and many other forms of communication between the sexes will not have been altered. Who and how will we educate and make changes in our main stream communications with one another when we have news channels and journalists, reporters, The White House tweets insulting anyone and everyone, sexist battles are played out on the national stage as we speak.

So if things are to really change out there in this world of super communication which ends up really being mixed up communications and misunderstandings, lots of insults and judgments, HOW exactly are we, will we be making anything a lasting and long term improvement?

I had to ask.

Chapter 18

The Climate Now 2017-2018

I had begun writing this book in 2013-2015 and while in the editing stages I put this book on the back burner in order to write two other books which seemed more urgent based on the subject matter and the ages of the people I wanted to interview. Of course not much has really changed since the end of 2015 except we are having a conversation about change once again.

I was awake at 3:00 a.m. February 2018 with this subject on my mind. If I were to read it out loud to you and if I was able to emphasize and put pauses in how I wrote it that would help you understand my meaning better – but here it is, this is what I wrote:

So what we now know and what we have always known is that people in general in some instances women, but mostly men over time have behaved badly and in fact have no real idea how to behave when it comes to appropriate behavior towards the opposite sex.

Most would say common sense should rule on the side of conservatism and respect. That most humans who have lived on the planet would eventually learn that women do not like to be cat called, yelled at, joked with sarcastically about most things sexual and certainly not in the workplace, that in fact boundaries do exist, have existed forever unbeknownst to many men, and most assuredly those men who have not or may not or will not ever grow up. Those men are the ones who after the age of about 20 should truly know better than to use words like girl when referring to women, who should know never to use the word Ma'am for any female over the age of 12 (maybe 10), and who should know never to say pussy or whuss to each other or to ever say those words to a female.

Of course I can turn this essay into a very long list of rants about what men should never do over the age of 20, (maybe 15) if they are to grow up to be an educated man in terms of how to respectfully treat a woman. Maybe in some ways we as a society ALL need to take responsibility for the fact and the idea that we have not truly put together a real instruction manual about how we are demanding to be treated currently.

If men learn from one another it is no wonder there are so many young males, teens, young men, and then even middle aged men who missed all of the common courtesy's we should all be aware of when it comes to always thinking about the long term, (that your behavior may come back to haunt you in the end), and that it does matter every day how you act, what you say, and how others may see you and judge what kind of a man you are and have become.

I am certain that the men who have behaved badly for the last 40 years began to shake in their collective boots, loafers, golf shoes, you name it. They shut their eyes tightly, hanging on while the wind has been blowing, hoping it would not come their way and their names would not be called. Whew, some may be prematurely saying now. Maybe whoever I treated badly years ago will keep quiet or will have forgotten. There are some who had behaved badly for 20 years and others who had just begun to wield their power and control just learning the best ways to try to use women as a means to an end, their end. We can only hope they are listening and instead of thinking we are cunts and bitches because we are telling our truth, maybe just maybe someone will hear the real truth. It is NOT OK to treat another human being as though she does not matter thinking she should comply with whatever sexual demands you may have because you take advantage of her youth, her innocence many times and her compliance that was taught to her by our society about not rocking the boat, being a "good girl" and going along with the status quo which should have been DEAD long ago.

I am certain many men are wondering what is all the fuss about? They are thinking I did not do this; I did not do anything wrong. There are good men on this planet, thank god. The ones who have always behaved, the ones who try to rein in other men they have witnessed behaving badly I say thank you to them. The others who stood by knowing this has been wrong, but had the "boys will be boys' attitude" You knew better and did nothing. Time truly is up. Women are tired.

There is a line from On Golden Pond where Katherine Hepburn says "bore, bore, bore aren't you tired of it all? WE ARE collectively, entirely tired of it all. PLEASE hear us. Please check your own words, your own behaviors and your own habits because EVERY DAY it matters. Be kind and be the best version of yourself you can be. Most of the time the struggle women face is exhausting. We walk a tight rope every day to have a career, respect from peers for a job well done, fewer accolades, less pay, more worry, more juggling of life's endless activities that often fall on a woman's plate. WE do in fact make "IT" all go. So stop the patriarchal egotistic I must be in charge and you must do what I say attitude. Join us on an equal platform because we ARE smart, we have very fine brains that are logical and scientific, and we have stamina to get the job done whatever and wherever that may be. And you know it. And it is alright and it will be. We can also still be everything to an equal partner in life, in the work place and as HUMANS on this planet. Half the world is watching.

Find a good counselor or therapist to help you negotiate asking for change in your relationship if you think it is salvageable. If you find yourself in a situation that will never change, consider leaving it. You and your counselor can discuss options. Find a way to realize that you are a wonderful human being who deserves the best from other people, the best of what they have to give not the worst. Find ways to repair and enhance your own self-esteem and self-love. There are support groups as well as the individual counseling that I advocate. Get busy healing, discovering and living.

Get involved in causes supporting positive changes for women. Be informed about the ways you can help to make a change in your community, in the lives of girls in your community.

Become a mentor, volunteer in women's organizations or in men's organizations. Men's clubs are no longer just for men. Soroptimist, Rotary, Kiwanis. There are many places you can help. I will list below some of the great websites to go to that tell about organizations that exist and work towards equality around the world every day. What I am advocating here is that by helping other women you are really helping yourself at the same time. If you have been a victim of domestic abuse of any kind, part of the healing process can be obtained by helping others.

I am also listing places a woman can call in the case of domestic abuse and the places you can find help in your community. I repeat, find a good counselor to talk to who can help you make changes in your life and in some cases change your situation. There are ways to be able to see a counselor even if it is difficult to afford. There are counselors who charge at reduced rates or on a sliding scale in order to help women in any income bracket.

A reminder for myself and to you the nice reader of this book. I have only touched on the subjects that have everything to do with gender exclusion, discrimination and abuse as well as the seemingly never ending story of women's fight for justice and equality in the world. I have tried to make this easy to read and digest especially for a younger audience of women who may have been as naïve as I was. I was there in the late 60's and early 70's and was proud of what we were saying and doing to bring these issues to the forefront. I am still proud of all of the women who were and are my role models.

One could write volumes, and many have about our fight for equality now in the 21st century. I find I have much more to say (as you can imagine lol) and will take this on in the future. I am hopeful that the information here helps in some way along your journey. As women now make headway in this ongoing saga I will be watching, I will be proud and we will move forward together. There is much more to be done. Don't let it wait.

A final few words about Narcissistic Abuse. "It is a dark and confusing tunnel where victims might spend years not realizing what is happening, unaware that their abuser has maliciously and intentionally created a world to isolate, demoralize, and dehumanize their victims to better feed and supply their disorder." I think there are many situations out there in the world between men and women like what is described here. Some behaviors may not be as extreme as described some are worse. If you see yourself and your relationship in these pages do not wait to make the necessary changes.

Although

The world is full of

suffering, it is also

full of overcoming it.

Helen Keller

Lists of services for women locally and in the United States

South Lake Tahoe, California

Local Domestic Violence Help and Shelter - http://liveviolencefree.org

Live Violence Free provides expansive services that directly benefit the health and well-being of our communities' families.

- Emergency Domestic Violence Shelter for up to 90 days.

- Advocacy and or accompaniment through legal and medical proceedings.

- 24 hour crisis hotline and crisis intervention counseling.

- Response team services with law enforcement, district attorney and hospital staff.

- Individual counseling for adults and children.

- Weekly support groups for survivors of domestic violence and sexual assault.

- Child abuse prevention education in local area schools.

- 80 hour crisis intervention certification course (required for all staff and volunteers).

- Emergency clothing, food and transportation.

- Referrals to other social service providers and local government agencies.

Peer Support, Advocacy and Accompaniment

Live Violence Free provides peer support for our clients through both our business office and 24-hour crisis line. Clients are provided with a listening ear to discuss their situation with someone who is supportive and non-judgmental. Clients may also receive advocacy and accompaniment for issues related to domestic violence.

Domestic Violence Support Group

A weekly, drop-in support group for women who have experienced violence in their lives. Our support groups are available in both English and Spanish. The goal of these groups is to provide individuals with a safe place to share their feelings, fears and challenges, learn the components of a healthy relationship and help rebuild their self-esteem.

Individual Counseling

Our long-term counseling focuses on helping survivors recover from the trauma they have experienced and confront possible underlying problems such as substance abuse or mental health issues.

Emergency Shelter and Transitional Housing

The Emergency Shelter and Transitional Housing program provides clients with temporary housing assistance as well as intensive, individualized services including counseling and life skills training to help clients secure permanent housing and a violence-free lifestyle.

Community Outreach

Live Violence Free provides presentations, information and referrals in order to educate the community on issues of domestic violence.

Domestic Violence Response Team

The South Lake Tahoe Police Department, the Office of the District Attorney and Live Violence Free work collaboratively to provide coordinated response services for domestic violence victims.

Live Violence Free is the only provider of domestic violence and sexual assault services
from South Lake Tahoe west to Kyburz, CA, north to Placer County, CA and east to Douglas County, NV. - and is the only provider in all of Alpine County.
http://liveviolencefree.org

National Hotlines

National Domestic Violence Hotline
Staffed 24 hours a day by trained counselors who can provide crisis assistance and information about shelters, legal advocacy, health care centers, and counseling.

1-800-799-SAFE (7233)
1-800-787-3224 (TDD)

888-750-6444 National number Domestic Violence help

Futures Without Violence
100 Montgomery Street
Presidio
San Francisco, CA 94129
Phone: 415-678-5500
TTY: 800-595-4889
FAX: 415-529-2930

Futureswithoutviolence.org
E-mail: info@futureswithoutviolence.org

National Battered Women's Law Project
275 7th Avenue, Suite 1206
New York, NY 10001

Woman space Network to End Violence Against
Immigrant Women
1530 Brunswick Avenue
Lawrenceville, NJ 08648
Phone: 609-394-0136
24 Hour Mercer County Hotline: 609-394-9000
For counseling 609-394-2532 www.womanspace.org

http://womenspaceinc.org/help/ Oregon based

Oregon (541)485-6513 (800-281-2800 rings quite a few
times – don't give up!

Project Safe has a 24 hour hotline at 706-543-3331 or by
visiting http://www.project-safe.org they are located in
Georgia but they take calls from anywhere 24 hours

Need help?

If you or someone you know has experienced sexual assault or domestic violence you can call to speak to a counselor or be referred to local services:

- **National Sexual Assault Hotline**: 1-800-656-4673. For Male Survivors of childhood sexual abuse, visit 1in6's Online Support Line: 1in6.org/men/get-help
- **This number automatically routes your call to the nearest location where you live or where you are calling from**
- **National Domestic Violence Hotline**: 1-800-799-7233. To find local resources and information about domestic violence, search domesticshelters.org's online database.
- **Teen Dating Violence Hotline**: 1-866-331-9474 or **text 'loveis'** to 22522. www.loveisrespect.org
- www.thehotline.org
  National Domestic Hotline website help is available 24/7 365 days a year

Bibliography

"Human Rights." American Heritage Dictionary of the English Language, Fourth Edition copyright 2000 by Houghton Mifflin Company All rights reserved retrieved 2014

Kristof, Nicholas D. and WuDunn, Sheryl – Half the Sky – Turning Oppression Into Opportunity For Women Worldwide, New York, Vintage Books, 2009

Lindsey, Linda L. Musslewhite, Dickson, Edition 5 Gender Roles – A sociological Perspective. Boston, MA Pearson Education, Inc., publishing as Prentice Hall, 2011

Henslin, James M. Social Problems A Down to Earth Approach, Tenth Edition, New York, Allyn & Bacon, 2011.

Nasreen, Taslima, End Violence Against Women. No Country For Women, Nasreen Taslima, 6, Nov 2013 http://freethoughtblogs.com/taslima/2012/07/14/our-   Men

Zuniga, Marielena, "Caged Birds." Best for Women, September, October, November 2007 Page 12-17.

World Health Organization – Violence against women – Intimate partner and sexual violence against women - last update 23, October 2013 and 5, March 2018

http://www.who.int/mediacentre/factsheets/fs239/en/index.html
Retrieved 2015, 2018

www.victimsofcrime.org
http://www.joyfulheartfoundation.org/learn/domestic-violence
Retrieved June 2, 2014 and again March 5, 2018

http://liveviolencefree.org

Retrieved June 3, 2014 and March 5, 2018

Ault, Laurie (Chapters Copyrighted)
Uncomfortably Numb, Book 2013, 2014 thoughts and research written for this essay June 2014.

www.feministmajority.org
Retrieved 2013 and 2018

National Center for Victims of Crime Web. 7 December 2013 and March 2018
http://www.victimsofcrime.org/media/reporting-on-child-sexual-abuse/child-sexual-abuse-statistics

No More
www.nomore.org
Dallas Business Wire Annual Survey Reveals
Cycle of Domestic Violence Continues in
Generation Y

https://www.huffingtonpost.com/2012/12/20/delhi
-bus-gang-rape-victim-intestines-shocking-
details_n_2340721.html Retrieved again 5, March
2018 https://www.cbsnews.com/news/indian-
gang-rape-victim-dies-in-hospital/

Mary Kay, Inc.
McGee, Susan G.S. Article 20 Reasons Why She
Stays or as she says the article should be titled:
"Why some battered women sometimes stay for
varying periods of time." Retrieved 2014

Women's Suffrage in the United States,
http://en.m.wikipedia.org/wiki/Women's_suffrage
_in_the_United_States, Retrieved 9/18/2012

Elaine Weiss, Ed.D, Family and Friends Guide to
Domestic Violence – How to Listen, Talk and Take
Action

http://www.abuseandrelationships.org/Content/T
he_Con/gaslighting.html

**Essays sources and works cited for Sociology 103
paper Jensen Jeung Instructor, March 27, 2017**

Works Cited

"Human Rights". American Heritage Dictionary of the English Language, Fourth Edition copyright 2000 by Houghton Mifflin Company

Kristof, Nicholas D. and WuDunn, Sheryl – Half the Sky – Turning Oppression Into Opportunity For Women Worldwide, New York, Vintage Books, 2009

Lindsey, Linda L. Musslewhite, Dickson, Edition 5, Gender Roles – A sociological
 Perspective. Boston, MA Pearson Education, Inc., publishing as Prentice Hall, 2011

National Center For Victims of Crime Web. 7 December 2013
http://www.victimsofcrime.org/media/reporting-on-child-sexual-abuse/child-sexual-abuse-statistics

Henslin, James M. Social Problems A Down to Earth Approach, Tenth Edition, New York, Allyn & Bacon, 2011.

Sources

Nasreen, Taslima, End Violence Against Women. No Country For Women,
Nasreen Taslima, 6, Nov 2013
http://freethoughtblogs.com/taslima/2012/07/14/our-

Men
Retrieved 2015 and 2018

Zuniga, Marielena, "Caged Birds". Best for Women, September, October, November 2007 Page 12-17.

World Health Organization – Violence against women – Intimate partner and sexual violence against women - last update 23, October 2013 http://www.who.int/mediacentre/factsheets/fs239/en/index.html

Essay Psychology 103, Adulthood and Aging

Katie Guiney Olsen, Instructor June 7, 2014
Abusive Relationships – Domestic Violence

Works Cited

http://www.victimsofcrime.org

http://www.joyfulheartfoundation.org/learn/domestic-violence

Retrieved June 2, 2014 http://liveviolencefree.org

Ault, Laurie (Chapters Copyrighted)
Uncomfortably Numb, Book 2013, 2014, 2018

thoughts and research written for this essay June 2014.

Sources

World Health Organization – Violence against women – Intimate partner and sexual violence against women - last update 23, October 2013 http://www.who.int/mediacentre/factsheets/fs239/en/index.html

www.feministmajority.org

National Center for Victims of Crime Web. 7 December 2013 http://www.victimsofcrime.org/media/reporting-on-child-sexual-abuse/child-sexual-abuse-statistics

Essay English 103 Josh Fleming, Instructor December 11, 2013
The Inequality of Women, The Unspoken Issue – Civil Rights, Equal Rights and Human Rights The sources listed previously in the works cited and bibliography were used in addition to links from websites noted in the essay as well.

**Books recommended about women's issues –
Historical**

I wholeheartedly recommend the book by Kate Millett called Sexual Politics written in 1969-1970

Betty Friedan, The Feminine Mystique 1963 (Keep in mind it was 1963) prior to major acceptance of Gay or Lesbian women.

 https://www.ourbodiesourselves.org/history/

The Yellow Wallpaper by Charlotte Perkins Gilman

This website and project tell us about the achievements overlooked over time by women in American History, Authors: Amisha Padnani and Jessica Bennett, March 8, 2018 New York Times called:
O V E R L O O K E D

Since 1851, obituaries in The New York Times have been Dominated by white men. Now we're adding the stories of remarkable women.

It is updated and more will be shared over time.

https://www.nytimes.com/interactive/2018/obituaries/overlooked-margaret-abbott.html

More current offerings in books:

Through Women's Eyes An American History with documents by Carol DuBois and Lynn Dumenil

This book is currently used in Women's History Classes as the textbook. If I were to tell anyone that only wanted a brief understanding of how we got to this place in time I would suggest the two chapters as follows: Read the Chapter entitled Beyond The Feminine Mystique Women's Lives: 1945-1965 and then also read: Modern Feminism and American Society chapters about what happened 1965-1980. If you have no knowledge yet or even if you do on the time period and how society affected life for women, this chapter is about the history of the women's movement. This one chapter in itself should be very enlightening.

Gender Roles A Sociological Perspective By Linda L. Lindsey – This book breaks down pretty much everything one would want to know about our society and how gender roles play into or out of our lives. This book includes Nature versus Nurture, Gender and Health, Feminism and the Media, Sociological Perspectives on Gender Roles and so much more. It talks about different countries, religions and practices. This book if read from cover to cover will give one a greater understanding of the roles of women across the globe and how societies are set up. A great book!

Current Books recommendations list:

Get out of my crotch! A collection 21 Writers Respond to America's War on Women's Rights and Reproductive Health

A MUST read if you have not already:

> **Half The Sky** Kristof, Nicholas D. and WuDunn, Sheryl – Half the Sky – Turning Oppression Into Opportunity For Women Worldwide, New York, Vintage Books, 2009

> More current books written 2015 – Now

https://www.amazon.com/Still-Rise-Persistence-Phenomenal-Women-ebook/dp/B06WW54RQ4/ref=dp_kinw_strp_1

Still I Rise – The Persistence of Phenomenal Women by Marlene Wagman-Geller

We Should All Be Feminists by Chimamanda Ngozi Adichie – A New York Times Best Seller

The Book of Awesome Women: Boundary Breakers, Freedom Fighters, Sheroes and Female Firsts by Becca Anderson

There are so many more out there!

All of the books mentioned here can be found on Amazon and at book stores